SHAKESPEARE MADE EASY

MODERN ENGLISH VERSION
SIDE-BY-SIDE WITH FULL ORIGINAL TEXT

P9-CES-604

The Merchant of Venice

EDITED AND RENDERED INTO MODERN ENGLISH BY
Alan Durband

BARRON'S

First U.S. edition published 1985 by Barron's Educational Series, Inc.

Hutchinson & Co. (Publishers) Ltd
An imprint of the Hutchinson Publishing Group
17-21 Conway Street, London W1P 6JD

Hutchinson Publishing Group (Australia) Pty Ltd
PO Box 496, 16-22 Church Street, Hawthorne,
Melbourne, Victoria 3122

Hutchinson Group (NZ) Ltd
32-34 View Road, PO Box 40-086, Glenfield, Auckland 10

Hutchinson Group (SA) (Pty) Ltd
PO Box 337, Bergvlei 2012, South Africa

First published 1984
© Alan Durband 1984

All inquiries should be addressed to:
Barron's Educational Series, Inc.
250 Wireless Boulevard
Hauppauge, NY 11788
http://www.barronseduc.com

ISBN-13: 978-0-8120-3570-4
ISBN-10: 0-8120-3570-4

Library of Congress Catalog No. 84-28470

Library of Congress Cataloging in Publication Data
Shakespeare, William, 1564–1616.
     The Merchant of Venice.

     (Shakespeare made easy)
     Summary: Presents the original text of Shakespeare's play side by side with a modern
version, discusses the author and the theater of his time, and provides quizzes and other
study activities.
     1. Shakespeare, William, 1564–1616. Merchant of Venice.
2. Shakespeare, William, 1564–1616—Study and teaching.
[1. Shakespeare, William, 1564–1616. Merchant of Venice.
2. Plays. 3. Shakespeare, William, 1564–1616—Study and teaching.]
I. Durband, Alan. II. Title. III. Series: Shakespeare, William, 1564–1616.
Shakespare made easy.
PR2825.A25   1985   822.3'3   84-28470
ISBN 0-8120-3570-4

PRINTED IN THE UNITED STATES OF AMERICA

35 31 33 32 31

'Reade him, therefore; and againe, and againe: And if then you do not like him, surely you are in some danger, not to understand him. . . .'

John Hemming
Henry Condell

Preface to the 1623 Folio Edition

Shakespeare Made Easy

Titles in the series

Macbeth
The Merchant of Venice
Julius Caesar
Romeo and Juliet
Henry IV, Part I
A Midsummer Night's Dream
The Tempest
Twelfth Night
Hamlet
King Lear

Contents

Introduction

Shakespeare Made Easy is intended for readers approaching the plays for the first time, who find the language of Elizabethan poetic drama an initial obstacle to understanding and enjoyment. In the past, the only answer to the problem has been to grapple with the difficulties with the aid of explanatory footnotes (often missing when they are most needed) and a stern teacher. Generations of students have complained that "Shakespeare was ruined for me at school."

Usually a fuller appreciation of Shakespeare's plays comes in later life. Often the desire to read Shakespeare for pleasure and enrichment follows from a visit to the theater, where excellence of acting and production can bring to life qualities which sometimes lie dormant on the printed page.

Shakespeare Made Easy can never be a substitute for the original plays. It cannot possibly convey the full meaning of Shakespeare's poetic expression, which is untranslatable. *Shakespeare Made Easy* concentrates on the dramatic aspect, enabling the novice to become familiar with the plot and characters, and to experience one facet of Shakespeare's genius. To know and understand the central issues of each play is a sound starting point for further exploration and development.

Discretion can be used in choosing the best method to employ. One way is to read the original Shakespeare first, ignoring the modern version – or using it only when interest or understanding flags. Another way is to read the translation first, to establish confidence and familiarity with plot and characters.

Either way, cross-reference can be illuminating. The modern text can explain what is being said if Shakespeare's language is particularly complex or his expression antiquated. The Shakespeare text will show the reader of the modern paraphrase how much more can be expressed in poetry than in prose.

The use of *Shakespeare Made Easy* means that the newcomer need never be overcome by textual difficulties. From first to last, a measure of understanding is at hand – the key is provided for what has been a locked door to many students in the past. And as understanding grows, so an awareness develops of the potential of language as a vehicle for philosophic and moral expression, beauty and the abidingly memorable.

Even professional Shakespearean scholars can never hope to arrive at a complete understanding of the plays. Each critic, researcher, actor or producer merely adds a little to the work that has already been done, or makes fresh interpretations of the texts for new generations. For everyone, Shakespearean appreciation is a journey. *Shakespeare Made Easy* is intended to help with the first steps.

William Shakespeare

His life

William Shakespeare was born in Stratford-on-Avon, Warwick-shire, on April 23, 1564, the son of a prosperous wool and leather merchant. Very little is known of his early life. From parish records we know that he married Ann Hathaway in 1582, when he was eighteen, and she was twenty-six. They had three children, the eldest of whom died in childhood.

Between his marriage and the next thing we know about him, there is a gap of ten years. Probably he became a member of a traveling company of actors. By 1592 he had settled in London and had earned a reputation as an actor and playwright.

Theaters were then in their infancy. The first (called *The Theatre*) was built in 1576. Two more followed as the taste for theater grew: *The Curtain* in 1577 and *The Rose* in 1587. The demand for new plays naturally increased. Shakespeare probably earned a living adapting old plays and working in collaboration with others on new ones. Today we would call him a "freelance," since he was not permanently attached to one theater.

In 1594, a new company of actors, The Lord Chamberlain's Men, was formed, and Shakespeare was one of the shareholders. He remained a member throughout his working life. The company regrouped in 1603 and was renamed The King's Men, with James I as its patron.

Shakespeare and his fellow actors prospered. In 1598 they built their own theater, *The Globe*, which broke away from the traditional rectangular shape of the inn and its yard (the early home of traveling bands of actors). Shakespeare described it in *Henry V* as "this wooden O," because it was circular.

Many other theaters were built by investors eager to profit from the new enthusiasm for drama. *The Hope*, *The Fortune*,

The Red Bull and *The Swan* were all open-air "public" theaters. There were also many "private" (or indoor) theaters, one of which (*The Blackfriars*) was purchased by Shakespeare and his friends because the child actors who performed there were dangerous competitors. (Shakespeare denounces them in *Hamlet.*)

After writing some thirty-seven plays (the exact number is something which scholars argue about), Shakespeare retired to his native Stratford, wealthy and respected. He died on his birthday, in 1616.

His plays

Shakespeare's plays were not all published in his lifetime. None of them comes to us exactly as he wrote it.

In Elizabethan times, plays were not regarded as either literature or good reading matter. They were written at speed (often by more than one writer), performed perhaps ten or twelve times and then discarded. Fourteen of Shakespeare's plays were first printed in Quarto (17cm × 21cm) volumes, not all with his name as the author. Some were authorized (the "good" Quartos) and probably were printed from prompt copies provided by the theater. Others were pirated (the "bad" Quartos) by booksellers who may have employed shorthand writers or bought actors' copies after the run of the play had ended.

In 1623, seven years after Shakespeare's death, John Hemming and Henry Condell (fellow-actors and shareholders in The King's Men) published a collected edition of Shakespeare's works – thirty-six plays in all – in a Folio (21cm × 34cm) edition. From their introduction it would seem that they used Shakespeare's original manuscripts ("we have scarce received from him a blot in his papers") but the Folio volumes that still survive are not all exactly alike, nor are the plays printed as we know them today, with act and scene divisions and stage directions.

A modern edition of a Shakespeare play is the result of a great deal of scholarly research and editorial skill over several centuries. The aim is always to publish a text (based on the good and bad Quartos and the Folio editions) that most closely resembles what Shakespeare intended. Misprints have added to the problems, so some words and lines are pure guesswork. This explains why some versions of Shakespeare's plays differ from others.

His theater

The first playhouse built as such in Elizabethan London, constructed in 1576, was *The Theatre*. Its co-founders were John Brayne, an investor, and James Burbage, a carpenter turned actor. Like the six or seven "public" (or outdoor) theaters which followed it over the next thirty years, it was situated outside the city, to avoid conflict with the authorities. They disapproved of players and playgoing, partly on moral and political grounds, and partly because of the danger of spreading the plague. (There were two major epidemics during Shakespeare's lifetime, and on each occasion the theaters were closed for lengthy periods.)

The Theatre was a financial success, and Shakespeare's company performed there until 1598, when a dispute over the lease of the land forced Burbage to take down the building. It was re-created in Southwark, as *The Globe*, with Shakespeare and several of his fellow-actors as the principal shareholders.

By modern standards, *The Globe* was small. Externally, the octagonal building measured less than thirty meters across, but in spite of this it could accommodate an audience of between two and three thousand people. (The largest of the three theaters at the National Theatre complex in London today seats 1160.)

Performances were advertised by means of playbills posted around the city, and they took place during the hours of daylight when the weather was suitable. A flag flew to show that all was well, to save playgoers a wasted journey.

Interior of the Swan Theatre – from a pen and ink drawing made in 1596 (Mansell Collection)

At the entrance, a doorkeeper collected one penny (about 60 cents today) for admission to the "pit" – a name taken from the old inn-yards, where bear-baiting and cock-fighting were popular sports. This was the minimum charge for seeing a play. The "groundlings," as they were called, simply stood around the three sides of the stage, in the open air. Those who were better off could pay extra for a seat under cover. Stairs led from the pit to three tiers of galleries around the walls. The higher one went, the more one paid. The best seats cost one shilling (or $7 today). In theaters owned by speculators like Francis Langley and Philip Henslowe, half the gallery takings went to the landlord.

A full house might consist of 800 groundlings and 1500 in the galleries, with a dozen more exclusive seats on the stage itself for the gentry. A new play might run for between six and sixteen performances; the average was about ten. As there were no breaks between scenes, and no intervals, most plays could be performed in two hours. A trumpet sounded three times before the play began.

The acting company assembled in the Tiring House at the rear of the stage. This was where they attired (or dressed) themselves: not in costumes representing the period of the play, but in Elizabethan doublet and hose. All performances were therefore in modern dress, though no expense was spared to make the stage costumes lavish. The entire company was male. By law actresses were not allowed, and female roles were performed by boys.

Access to the stage from the Tiring House was through two doors, one on each side of the stage. Because there was no front curtain, every entrance had to have its corresponding exit, so an actor killed on stage had to be carried off. There was no scenery: the audience used its imagination, guided by the spoken word. Storms and night scenes might well be performed on sunny days in mid-afternoon; the Elizabethan playgoer relied entirely on the playwright's descriptive skills to establish the dramatic atmosphere.

Once on stage, the actors and their expensive clothes were protected from sudden showers by a canopy, the underside of which was painted blue and spangled with stars to represent the heavens. A trapdoor in the stage made ghostly entrances and the gravedigging scene in *Hamlet* possible. Behind the main stage, in between the two entrance doors, there was a curtained area, concealing a small inner stage, useful for bedroom scenes. Above this was a balcony, which served for castle walls (as in *Henry V*) or a domestic balcony (as in the famous scene in *Romeo and Juliet*).

The acting style in Elizabethan times was probably more declamatory than we favor today, but the close proximity of the audience also made a degree of intimacy possible. In those days soliloquies and asides seemed quite natural. Act and scene divisions did not exist (those in printed versions of the play today have been added by editors), but Shakespeare often indicates a scene ending by a rhyming couplet.

A company such as The King's Men at *The Globe* would consist of around twenty-five actors, half of whom might be shareholders, and the rest part-timers engaged for a particular play. Among the shareholders in *The Globe* were several specialists – William Kempe, for example, was a renowned comedian and Robert Armin was a singer and dancer. Playwrights wrote parts to suit the actors who were available, and devised ways of overcoming the absence of women. Shakespeare often has his heroines dress as young men, and physical contact between lovers was formal compared with the realism we expect today.

His verse

Shakespeare wrote his plays mostly in blank verse: that is, unrhymed lines consisting of ten syllables, alternately stressed and unstressed. The technical term for this form is the iambic pentameter. When Shakespeare first began to write for the stage, it was fashionable to maintain this regular beat from the first line of the play till the last.

Shakespeare conformed at first and then experimented. Some of his early plays contain whole scenes in rhyming couplets – in *Romeo and Juliet*, for example, there is extensive use of rhyme, and as if to show his versatility, Shakespeare even inserts a sonnet into the dialogue.

But as he matured, he sought greater freedom of expression than rhyme allowed. **Rhyme is still used to indicate a scene ending, or to stress lines which he wishes the audience to remember. Generally, though, Shakespeare moved toward the rhythms of everyday speech.** This gave him many dramatic advantages, which he fully and subtly exploits in terms of atmosphere, character, emotion, stress and pace.

It is Shakespeare's poetic imagery, however, that most distinguishes his verse from that of lesser playwrights. It enables him to stretch the imagination, express complex thought-patterns in **memorable language** and convey a number of associated ideas in a compressed and economical form. A study of Shakespeare's imagery – especially in his later plays – is often the key to a full understanding of his meaning and purposes.

At the other extreme is prose. Shakespeare normally reserves it for servants, clowns, commoners and pedestrian matters such as lists, messages and letters.

The Merchant of Venice

Date

The Merchant of Venice was written about 1596: we cannot date it precisely. It was first entered in the Stationers' Register in 1598 and first printed in 1600, in a Quarto edition published by Thomas Heyes. The Folio edition of 1623 uses the same text, but the editors added act and scene divisions and stage directions.

Source

Shakespeare may have reworked an existing play – or plays – on the same subject. This was a common practice in the Elizabethan theater and at this time Shakespeare was new to the craft of play-writing. Several plays on similar themes are known to have existed, though no copies have survived.

It is also possible that he found the basic stories of the pound of flesh and the rings in a collection of tales called *Il Pecorone* (written by a notary of Florence called Ser Giovanni in the fourteenth century and published in translation in 1558), and that he added the casket story from a work called the *Gesta Romanorum* (available to Shakespeare in a new translation dated 1577).

Shakespeare's knowledge of Jews would have been based entirely on hearsay. Neither he nor his audience would have met one, since Jews had been legally banned from Britain in the fourteenth century.

An exception seems to have been made in the case of a court physician called Roderigo Lopez, who was of Jewish descent. In 1598 he was hanged, drawn and quartered for high treason, having been found guilty, after a celebrated trial, of planning to poison Queen Elizabeth. There is a probable reference to this in

Act 4, *Scene 1*: Gratiano refers to a "a wolf who hanged for human slaughter." The Latin for wolf is "lupus" – the Elizabethan audience would have detected the pun.

Text

There is a good deal of textual evidence to show that *The Merchant of Venice* as we know it is not a printed version of Shakespeare's original manuscript. Many cuts seem to have been made – for example, the masque that is planned for over several scenes never takes place, though perhaps it did in Shakespeare's original draft, or earlier plays.

There is evidence of other revisions, all suggesting that the Heyes Quarto is based on a prompt copy. This would have been compiled by the company as a working document in the theater. Similar procedures are common today in theaters specializing in new work: producers and actors make changes after the delivery of an author's manuscript, often for purely practical reasons. This seems to have happened in the case of *The Merchant of Venice*.

The Merchant of Venice

Original text and modern version

The characters

The Duke of Venice
The Prince of Morocco ⎫ suitors to **Portia**
The Prince of Arragon ⎭
Antonio   a merchant of Venice
Bassanio   his friend
Gratiano ⎫
Solanio ⎬   friends of **Antonio** and **Bassanio**
Salerio ⎭
Lorenzo   in love with **Jessica**
Shylock   a Jew
Tubal   another Jew, and friend of **Shylock**
Lancelot Gobbo   servant to **Shylock** and later **Bassanio**
Old Gobbo   Lancelot's father
Leonardo   servant to **Bassanio**
Balthazar ⎫
Stephano ⎭   servants to **Portia**
Portia   a wealthy lady of Belmont
Nerissa   her waiting-maid
Jessica   **Shylock**'s daughter
Magnificoes of Venice, **Officers** of the Court of Justice, a
   Gaoler, **Servants** and **Attendants**

Act one

Scene 1

Venice. Enter **Antonio, Salerio,** *and* **Solanio.**

Antonio In sooth I know not why I am so sad:
It wearies me, you say it wearies you;
But how I caught it, found it, or came by it,
What stuff 'tis made of, whereof it is born,
5 I am to learn;
And such a want-wit sadness makes of me,
That I have much ado to know myself.

Salerio Your mind is tossing on the ocean;
There, where your argosies with portly sail –
10 Like signiors and rich burghers on the flood,
Or as it were the pageants of the sea –
Do overpeer the petty traffickers,
That curtsy to them, do them reverence,
As they fly by them with their woven wings.

15 **Solanio** Believe me, sir, had I such venture forth,
The better part of my affections would
Be with my hopes abroad. I should be still
Plucking the grass to know where sits the wind,
Peering in maps for ports and piers and roads:
20 And every object that might make me fear
Misfortune to my ventures, out of doubt,
Would make me sad.

Salerio   My wind, cooling my broth,
Would blow me to an ague when I thought
What harm a wind too great might do at sea.
25 I should not see the sandy hour-glass run

Act one

Scene 1

A wharf in Venice, Italy, in the sixteenth century. **Antonio,** *a rich merchant suffering from depression, is talking to two friends,* **Salerio** *and* **Solanio**.

Antonio [*sighing*] I really don't know why I'm in this mood. It wearies me. You find it tiresome too, you say. I don't know how I caught it, or found it, or acquired it, or what it's made of, or what brought it on. I feel so muddled in these moods, I just can't sort things out.

Salerio [*understandingly*] Your mind is tossing on the ocean. It's out there [*pointing toward the sea*] where your treasure ships, with billowing sails — like stout aristocrats and rich citizens of the waves, or like colorful spectacles of the sea! — tower above the common working boats, which bow respectfully as they fly past, speeded by the wind.

Solanio Believe me, sir, if I'd taken such risks, most of my thoughts would be abroad with my investments. I'd be plucking blades of grass to see which way the wind blows, poring over maps for ports, and piers, and safe anchorages. Anything that could endanger my ventures would depress me.

Salerio As I blew on my soup to cool it, I'd catch a chill through thinking of the harm a stormy wind might do at sea. Every time I saw an hourglass, the running sand would make me

But I should think of shallows and of flats,
And see my wealthy Andrew docked in sand,
Vailing her high-top lower than her ribs
To kiss her burial. Should I go to church
30   And see the holy edifice of stone,
And not bethink me straight of dangerous rocks,
Which touching but my gentle vessel's side
Would scatter all her spices on the stream,
Enrobe the roaring waters with my silks,
35   And, in a word, but even now worth this,
And now worth nothing? Shall I have the thought
To think on this, and shall I lack the thought
That such a thing bechanced would make me sad?
But tell not me; I know Antonio
40   Is sad to think upon his merchandise.

Antonio   Believe me, no – I thank my fortune for it –
My ventures are not in one bottom trusted,
Nor to one place; nor is my whole estate
Upon the fortune of this present year:
45   Therefore my merchandise makes me not sad.

Solanio   Why then you are in love.

Antonio   Fie, fie!

Solanio   Not in love neither? then let us say you are sad
Because you are not merry; and 'twere as easy
For you to laugh and leap, and say you are merry,
50   Because you are not sad. Now, by two-headed Janus,
Nature hath framed strange fellows in her time:
Some that will evermore peep through their eyes,
And laugh like parrots at a bag-piper;
And other of such vinegar aspect,
55   That they'll not show their teeth in way of smile,
Though Nestor swear the jest be laughable.

[*Enter* **Bassanio, Lorenzo,** *and* **Gratiano**]

think of shallow water and sandbanks. I'd imagine my precious ship *Andrew* grounded in sand, her topsails lowered as if at a funeral. I couldn't go to church without the holy stones reminding me of dangerous rocks. They'd only have to scrape my fragile vessel's side to scatter her cargo of spices into the water and clothe the raging seas with my silk cloths. One moment I'd be rich. The next, a pauper. Can I imagine this but fail to appreciate that if it happened I'd be miserable? You can't fool me! Antonio must be worrying about his goods.

Antonio   [*shaking his head*] No, I assure you. I'm lucky. Not all my investments are in one ship or in one place. My fortune doesn't depend on this year's trading. So I'm not depressed about my merchandise.

Solanio   [*teasing*] Well, then, you must be in love!

Antonio   [*protesting*] Now really!

Solanio   Not in love either? Then let's say [*trying to be helpful*] you are sad because you are not merry. And you could be laughing and frollicking about if you wanted to, pretending to be merry, because you are not really sad. [*Explaining*] By Janus – whose two heads faced in opposite directions! – Nature has made some peculiar people in her time. Some are permanently wreathed in smiles. They'd laugh like idiots at the mournful moan of a bagpiper. And then there are the vinegary types. They wouldn't crack their faces into a smile, even if some grave old graybeard said the joke was funny!

[*Enter* **Bassanio**, *a young gentleman, and his friends* **Lorenzo** *and* **Gratiano**]

Here comes Bassanio, your most noble kinsman,
Gratiano, and Lorenzo. Fare ye well,
We leave you now with better company.

60 **Salerio**   I would have stayed till I had made you merry,
If worthier friends had not prevented me.

Antonio   Your worth is very dear in my regard.
I take it your own business calls on you,
And you embrace th'occasion to depart.

65 **Salerio**   Good morrow, my good lords.

Bassanio   Good signiors both, when shall we laugh? say,
when?
You grow exceeding strange: must it be so?

Salerio   We'll make our leisures to attend on yours.

[*Exeunt* **Salerio** *and* **Solanio**]

Lorenzo   My Lord Bassanio, since you have found Antonio,
70 We two will leave you, but at dinner-time
I pray you have in mind where we must meet.

Bassanio   I will not fail you.

Gratiano   You look not well, Signior Antonio,
You have too much respect upon the world:
75 They lose it that do buy it with much care:
Believe me you are marvellously changed.

Antonio   I hold the world but as the world, Gratiano –
A stage, where every man must play a part,
And mine a sad one.

Gratiano   Let me play the fool,
80 With mirth and laughter let old wrinkles come,
And let my liver rather heat with wine,

Here's your kinsman Bassanio, with Gratiano and Lorenzo. [*Seeing his chance to go*] Goodbye, then. We'll leave you in better company.

Salerio   [*also taking advantage of the opportunity*] I'd have stayed to cheer you up if worthier friends hadn't forestalled me.

Antonio   [*understandingly*] That's good of you but you have your own business to attend to. This gives you the chance to slip away.

Salerio   [*to the newcomers*] Good morning, my lords.

Bassanio   [*greeting them genially*] Gentlemen both! When shall we have a good laugh together, eh? Well, when? You're almost strangers. Must you be?

Salerio   [*anxious to get away*] We must fix a time to meet you.

[**Salerio** *and* **Solanio** *bow politely and depart*]

Lorenzo   Bassanio, now you've found Antonio, we'll leave you. Don't forget we are meeting for dinner.

Bassanio   I won't let you down!

Gratiano   You don't look well, Signior Antonio. You let things get on top of you. Worrying gains you nothing. Believe me, you are a different man nowadays.

Antonio   I take the world for what it is, Gratiano. It's a stage, on which every man has a part to play. Mine happens to be a sad one.

Gratiano   I want to be the clown, then! Let mirth and laughter make my wrinkles. And may wine warm me up, not sighs cool

Than my heart cool with mortifying groans.
Why should a man, whose blood is warm within,
Sit like his grandsire cut in alabaster?
85 Sleep when he wakes and creep into the jaundice
By being peevish? I tell thee what, Antonio –
I love thee, and 'tis my love that speaks –
There are a sort of men whose visages
Do cream and mantle like a standing pond,
90 And do a wilful stillness entertain,
With purpose to be dressed in an opinion
Of wisdom, gravity, profound conceit,
As who should say, 'I am Sir Oracle,
And when I ope my lips let no dog bark.'
95 O, my Antonio, I do know of these
That therefore only are reputed wise
For saying nothing; when, I am very sure,
If they should speak, would almost damn those ears
Which, hearing them, would call their brothers fools.
100 I'll tell thee more of this another time.
But fish not with this melancholy bait
For this fool gudgeon, this opinion.
Come, good Lorenzo. Fare ye well awile,
I'll end my exhortation after dinner.

105 **Lorenzo**   Well, we will leave you then till dinner-time.
I must be one of these same dumb wise men,
For Gratiano never lets me speak.

Gratiano   Well, keep me company but two years more,
Thou shalt not know the sound of thine own tongue.

110 **Antonio**   Fare you well. I'll grow a talker for this gear.

Gratiano   Thanks, i'faith – for silence is only commendable
In a neat's tongue dried, and a maid not vendible.

[*Exeunt* **Gratiano** *and* **Lorenzo**]

me down! Why should a warm-blooded man behave like a
stone-cold statue of his grandfather? Wake up to doze his days
away? Turn sallow with peevishness? I'll tell you what,
Antonio – and I speak out of friendship – there are some men
who have deadpan faces. They cultivate silence, the idea
being to seem wise, grave and astute, as though to say, "I
am Sir Knowall. When I speak, no dog should dare to bark!"
Antonio, I know some men whose reputation for wisdom is
based on saying nothing. If they did open their mouths, they'd
sound very stupid and invite ridicule. More of this some
other time! But don't you go fishing for this phony reputation
with melancholy as your bait. Come on, Lorenzo. [*To* **Antonio**]
Farewell for now. I'll finish my sermon after dinner.

Lorenzo   Right. [*He bows*] We'll leave you till dinnertime, then.
[*To* **Antonio**] I must be one of those same dumb wise men, for
Gratiano never lets me get a word in!

Gratiano   Be my friend for two more years, and you'll have
forgotten the sound of your own voice!

Antonio   [*to* **Gratiano**] Goodbye. I suppose I'd better start
talking, then.

Gratiano   If you please. Silence is only a virtue in dried ox
tongues and old maids!

[**Gratiano** *and* **Lorenzo** *leave in high spirits*]

Antonio   Is that any thing now?

Bassanio   Gratiano speaks an infinite deal of nothing, more
115   than any man in all Venice. His reasons are as two grains of
wheat hid in two bushels of chaff: you shall seek all day ere
you find them, and when you have them they are not worth
the search.

Antonio   Well, tell me now what lady is the same
120   To whom you swore a secret pilgrimage,
That you today promised to tell me of?

Bassanio   'Tis not unknown to you, Antonio,
How much I have disabled mine estate,
By something showing a more swelling port
125   Than my faint means would grant continuance:
Nor do I now make moan to be abridged
From such a noble rate; but my chief care
Is to come fairly off from the great debts
Wherein my time, something too prodigal,
130   Hath left me gaged. To you, Antonio,
I owe the most in money and in love,
And from your love I have a warranty
To unburthen all my plots and purposes
How to get clear of all the debts I owe.

135 **Antonio**   I pray you, good Bassanio, let me know it;
And if it stand, as you yourself still do,
Within the eye of honour, be assured,
My purse, my person, my extremest means,
Lie all unlocked to your occasions.

140 **Bassanio**   In my school-days, when I had lost one shaft,
I shot his fellow of the self-same flight
The self-same way, with more advised watch,
To find the other forth, and by adventuring both,
I oft found both: I urge this childhood proof,
145   Because what follows is pure innocence.

Antonio   What do you make of that?

Bassanio   [*laughing*] Gratiano talks more rubbish than any other man in Venice. The sense in what he says is like two grains of wheat hidden in a bushel of chaff. You could spend all day looking for them. And when you'd found them, they wouldn't be worth the search!

Antonio   Well, now, Bassanio. Who's this lady who has taken your fancy? You promised you'd tell me today.

Bassanio   [*serious now*] Antonio, you well know how I squandered my inheritance by living above my means. I'm not complaining, now that I have to cut back. My ambition is to repay the large debts my extravagant living left me burdened with. I owe most to you, in money and in affection. And because of that affection, I feel I can speak freely about my plans and schemes to rid myself of debts.

Antonio   Tell me everything, Bassanio. If the scheme is honorable – as you still are – my wallet, myself and all my resources are at your service.

Bassanio   [*explaining*] In my schooldays, if I lost an arrow, I shot another in exactly the same way, watching its flight very carefully, to see where the first fell. By risking both, I often found both. I quote this childhood story because what I'm going to propose is just as artless. I owe you a great deal and –

I owe you much, and, like a wilful youth,
That which I owe is lost; but if you please
To shoot another arrow that self way
Which you did shoot the first, I do not doubt,
150 As I will watch the aim, or to find both,
Or bring your latter hazard back again,
And thankfully rest debtor for the first.

Antonio   You know me well, and herein spend but time
To wind about my love with circumstance,
155 And out of doubt you do me now more wrong
In making question of my uttermost
Than if you had made waste of all I have:
Then do but say to me what I should do
That in your knowledge may by me be done,
160 And I am prest unto it: therefore, speak.

Bassanio   In Belmont is a lady richly left,
And she is fair, and, fairer than that word,
Of wondrous virtues: sometimes from her eyes
I did receive fair speechless messages.
165 Her name is Portia, nothing undervalued
To Cato's daughter, Brutus' Portia;
Nor is the wide world ignorant of her worth,
For the four winds blow in from every coast
Renowned suitors, and her sunny locks
170 Hang on her temples like a golden fleece,
Which makes her seat of Belmont Colchos' strand,
And many Jasons come in quest of her.
O my Antonio, had I but the means
To hold a rival place with one of them,
175 I have a mind presages me such thrift,
That I should questionless be fortunate.

Antonio   Thou know'st that all my fortunes are at sea;
Neither have I money nor commodity
To raise a present sum: therefore go forth,

blame my youth – what I owe is lost. But if you would shoot another arrow in the same direction as the first, I've no doubt (because I'll watch things carefully this time) that I'll either find both, or return the second back to you, and gratefully stand by the debt I owed you in the first place.

Antonio   You know me well enough. You've no need to spend precious time making out a special case. Doubting I would back you unreservedly hurts more than squandering my fortune! Just say what you'd like me to do that I can do, and I'm at your service. Tell me more.

Bassanio   In Belmont there is a rich heiress. She is beautiful. And what's better, she has wonderful qualities. She has shown by her looks that she favors me. She is called Portia – no way inferior to Cato's daughter, Portia, the one who married Brutus. Not that the world at large is ignorant of her worthiness. Famous suitors come from the four corners of the earth. Her fair hair is the Golden Fleece that attracts many Jasons to the Belmont shore. Oh, Antonio – I feel convinced I'd be successful if only I had the money to make myself a rival!

Antonio   You know all my wealth is tied up in cargoes. I haven't the ready cash, or things to sell, to raise the money now. So go

180   Try what my credit can in Venice do:
       That shall be racked, even to the uttermost,
       To furnish thee to Belmont, to fair Portia.
       Go, presently inquire, and so will I,
       Where money is, and I no question make
185   To have it of my trust or for my sake.

                                                    [*Exeunt*]

Scene 2

A room in Portia's house at Belmont. Enter **Portia** *and her waiting-woman* **Nerissa**.

Portia   By my troth, Nerissa, my little body is aweary of this
great world.

Nerissa   You would be, sweet madam, if your miseries were in
the same abundance as your good fortunes are: and yet for
5   aught I see, they are as sick that surfeit with too much as they
that starve with nothing; it is no mean happiness therefore to
be seated in the mean: superfluity comes sooner by white
hairs, but competency lives longer.

Portia   Good sentences, and well pronounced.

10 **Nerissa**   They would be better if well followed.

Portia   If to do were as easy as to know what were good to do,
chapels had been churches, and poor men's cottages princes'
palaces. It is a good divine that follows his own instructions! I
can easier teach twenty what were good to be done, than be
15   one of the twenty to follow mine own teaching. The brain may
devise laws for the blood, but a hot temper leaps o'er a cold

and see what my credit is good for in Venice. Stretch it to the utmost to finance your trip to Belmont and the beautiful Portia. Go at once and ask around. I'll do the same. See where money is to be had. Borrow it on the strength of my credit or my personal friendships – I don't mind.

[*They go in search of* **Bassanio's** *loan*]

Scene 2

The hall of **Portia's** *house at Belmont.* **Portia** *is sitting talking to her maid,* **Nerissa**.

Portia   [*sighing*] Honestly, Nerissa, my little body is weary of this great world.

Nerissa   You would be, dear madam, if you had as much misery as you have good fortune. As far as I can tell, you can be just as sick through over eating as you can be from starving. There's a lot to be said for being poor. Excess makes you old before your time. You live longer if you take things in moderation.

Portia   Admirable sentiments, and well spoken!

Nerissa   They'd be better if they were followed . . .

Portia   If practicing were as easy as preaching, chapels would be churches and poor men's cottages would be princes' palaces. It's a good cleric who follows his own advice. I'd rather instruct twenty people how best to behave, than be one of the twenty obliged to follow my teaching. Reason tries to control behavior, but hot passions ignore the rules. Madcap

decree: such a hare is madness the youth, to skip o'er the
meshes of good counsel the cripple. But this reasoning is not
in the fashion to choose me a husband. O me, the word
20 'choose'! I may neither choose whom I would nor refuse
whom I dislike; so is the will of a living daughter curbed by
the will of a dead father. Is it not hard, Nerissa, that I cannot
choose one, nor refuse none?

Nerissa   Your father was ever virtuous, and holy men at their
25 death have good inspiration: therefore the lottery that he hath
devised in these three chests of gold, silver and lead, whereof
who chooses his meaning chooses you, will no doubt never be
chosen by any rightly, but one whom you shall rightly love.
But what warmth is there in your affection towards any of
30 these princely suitors that are already come?

Portia   I pray thee over-name them, and as thou namest them,
I will describe them, and according to my description level at
my affection.

Nerissa   First there is the Neapolitan prince.

35 **Portia**   Ay, that's a colt indeed, for he doth nothing but talk of
his horse, and he makes it a great appropriation to his own
good parts that he can shoe him himself. I am much afeard my
lady his mother played false with a smith.

Nerissa   Then is there the County Palatine.

40 **Portia**   He doth nothing but frown, as who should say, 'An you
will not have me, choose!': he hears merry tales, and smiles
not: I fear he will prove the weeping philosopher when he
grows old, being so full of unmannerly sadness in his youth. I
had rather be married to a death's-head with a bone in his
45 mouth than to either of these: God defend me from these two!

Nerissa   How say you by the French lord, Monsieur Le Bon?

youth rejects good advice, because it's a handicap. But all this philosophizing won't help me to choose a husband. Oh, dear! [*She sighs again*] That word "choose." I can neither make my own choice nor turn down those I dislike. So the will of a living daughter is thwarted by the will of a dead father. Isn't it unfair, Nerissa, that I can't either choose or refuse?

Nerissa   Your father was very virtuous, and on their deathbeds, holy men are frequently inspired. Therefore the lottery he devised of the three chests – one of gold, one of silver, and one of lead, with you as the prize for the correct choice – will no doubt make sure that only the right man will provide the right answer. How do you feel about the princely suitors who have already arrived?

Portia   Run over their names, please, and as you call them out, I'll describe them. Then you can guess how I feel about them.

Nerissa   First, there's the Neapolitan prince.

Portia   Now there's a frisky youngster! He can talk about nothing but his horse. He thinks he deserves full marks for being able to shoe him himself. I suspect his mother had an affair with a blacksmith!

Nerissa   Then there's the Count Palatine.

Portia   He frowns all the time, as if to say, "If you won't marry me, you can please yourself!" He listens to jokes but never smiles. He'll be a prophet of doom in his old age, he's so full of wretched misery in his youth. I'd rather be married to a death's-head than to either of these. God save me from them both!

Nerissa   How do you like the French gentleman, Monsieur Le Bon?

Portia   God made him, and therefore let him pass for a man. In truth, I know it is a sin to be a mocker, but he! why, he hath a horse better than the Neapolitan's, a better bad habit of
50   frowning than the Count Palatine; he is every man in no man; if a throstle sing, he falls straight a capering; he will fence with his own shadow. If I should marry him, I should marry twenty husbands. If he would despise me I would forgive him, for if he love me to madness, I shall never requite him.

55 **Nerissa**   What say you then to Falconbridge, the young baron of England?

Portia   You know I say nothing to him, for he understands not me, nor I him: he hath neither Latin, French, nor Italian, and you will come into the court and swear that I have a poor
60   pennyworth in the English. He is a proper man's picture, but, alas! who can converse with a dumb-show? How oddly he is suited! I think he bought his doublet in Italy, his round hose in France, his bonnet in Germany, and his behaviour every where.

65 **Nerissa**   What think you of the Scottish lord, his neighbour?

Portia   That he hath a neighbourly charity in him, for he borrowed a box of the ear of the Englishman, and swore he would pay him again when he was able: I think the Frenchman became his surety, and sealed under for another.

70 **Nerissa**   How like you the young German, the Duke of Saxony's nephew?

Portia   Very vilely in the morning when he is sober, and most vilely in the afternoon when he is drunk: when he is best, he is a little worse than a man, and when he is worst, he is little
75   better than a beast. An the worst fall that ever fell, I hope I shall make shift to go without him.

Portia   [*raising her eyes*] Well, God made him, so we won't argue about his manhood. Honestly, I know it's wicked to mock, but him! His horse is better than the Neapolitan's. He frowns better than the Count Palatine. He's everybody—and nobody. If a thrush sings, he dances. He'd fence with his own shadow. If I married him, I'd be marrying twenty husbands. I wouldn't mind if he hated me. I certainly couldn't return his love if he adored me to distraction!

Nerissa   Well, then, what about Falconbridge, the English baron?

Portia   You know I never say anything to him. He doesn't understand me, and I don't understand him. He speaks neither Latin, French nor Italian, and you'll bear witness that I'm pretty lacking in English. He looks manly enough, but who could converse with a dummy? And how queerly he dresses! I think he got his vest in Italy, his breeches and stockings in France, his hat in Germany and his behavior everywhere.

Nerissa   What do you think of his neighbor, the Scottish lord?

Portia   That he has neighborly charity. The Englishman boxed his ears. Like a good neighbor, the Scottish lord promised to repay him as soon as he could. I think the Frenchman took his part – guaranteeing him another beating!

Nerissa   How do you like the young German – the Duke of Saxony's nephew?

Portia   I detest him in the morning when he's sober and loathe him in the evening when he's drunk. At his best, he's less than a man. At his worst, he's little better than a beast. If the worst ever happened, I trust I could manage without him.

Nerissa If he should offer to choose, and choose the right casket, you should refuse to perform your father's will, if you should refuse to accept him.

80 **Portia** Therefore, for fear of the worst, I pray thee set a deep glass of Rhenish wine on the contrary casket, for if the devil be within, and that temptation without, I know he will choose it. I will do any thing, Nerissa, ere I will be married to a sponge.

85 **Nerissa** You need not fear, lady, the having any of these lords: they have acquainted me with their determinations, which is indeed to return to their home, and to trouble you with no more suit, unless you may be won by some other sort than your father's imposition depending on the caskets.

90 **Portia** If I live to be as old as Sibylla, I will die as chaste as Diana, unless I be obtained by the manner of my father's will. I am glad this parcel of wooers are so reasonable, for there is not one among them but I dote on his very absence: and I pray God grant them a fair departure.

95 **Nerissa** Do you not remember, lady, in your father's time, a Venetian, a scholar and a soldier, that came hither in company of the Marquis of Montferrat?

Portia Yes, yes, it was Bassanio, as I think so was he called.

Nerissa True, madam, he, of all the men that ever my foolish
100 eyes looked upon, was the best deserving a fair lady.

Portia I remember him well, and I remember him worthy of thy praise.

[*Enter a* **Servant**]

How now! what news?

Servant The four strangers seek for you, madam, to take their
105 leave: and there is a forerunner come from a fifth, the Prince

Nerissa   If he offers to choose and he chooses the right casket, you would be going against your father's will if you refused to marry him.

Portia   Therefore, to prevent the worst, I'd be obliged if you would set a large glass of Rhine wine on the wrong casket. He'd be tempted to choose that one even if the devil were hidden inside. I'll do anything, Nerissa, rather than marry a sponge!

Nerissa   Madam, you needn't worry about having any of these lords. They've told me their intentions. They propose to return home and to court you no further, unless you can be won by some other means than your father's device of the caskets.

Portia   If I should live to be as old as the ancient Sybilla, I'll die as chaste as the virginal Diana unless I'm wooed in accordance with my father's will. I'm glad this collection of suitors is so reasonable. There's not one of them whose absence I don't adore. May God grant them a speedy farewell!

Nerissa   Do you remember, madam, when your father was alive, a Venetian, a scholar and a soldier, who came here in the Marquis of Montferrat's company?

Portia   Yes, yes! That was Bassanio, I think he was called.

Nerissa   That's right, madam. Of all the men my foolish eyes have ever seen, he was the most deserving of an attractive lady.

Portia   I remember him well, and he deserves your praise.

[*A* **Servant** *enters*]

Well, what news?

Servant   The four strangers are looking for you, madam, to say goodbye. A messenger has arrived from a fifth – the Prince of of Morocco, who brings word the prince his master will be here tonight.

Portia   If I could bid the fifth welcome with so good heart as I can bid the other four farewell, I should be glad of his
110   approach: if he have the condition of a saint and the complexion of a devil, I had rather he should shrive me than wive me.
Come, Nerissa. Sirrah, go before.
Whiles we shut the gate upon one wooer, another knocks at
115   the door.

[Exeunt]

Scene 3

A street in Venice. Enter **Bassanio** *and* **Shylock**.

Shylock   Three thousand ducats; well.

Bassanio   Ay, sir, for three months.

Shylock   For three months; well.

Bassanio   For the which, as I told you, Antonio shall be
5   bound.

Shylock   Antonio shall become bound; well.

Bassanio   May you stead me? Will you pleasure me? Shall I know your answer?

Shylock   Three thousand ducats for three months; and
10   Antonio bound.

Bassanio   Your answer to that.

Morocco – to say he will be here tonight.

Portia   If I could greet the fifth as heartily as I can bid the other four farewell, I'd be glad of his arrival. Should he have the character of a saint, but the looks of a devil, I'd rather he blessed me than wedding-dressed me. Come on, Nerissa. [*To the* **Servant**] Go on ahead. [*Sighing*] We no sooner slam the door on one wooer than another knocks on it!

[*They leave*]

Scene 3

A street in Venice, outside Shylock's house. **Bassanio** *and* **Shylock** *are negotiating a loan.*

Shylock   [*as he writes*] Three thousand ducats [gold coins]. [*To* **Bassanio**] Well . . .

Bassanio   Yes, sir. For three months.

Shylock [*writing*] For three months. [*Looking up again*] Well . . .

Bassanio   For which, as I said, Antonio will stand guarantor.

Shylock [*making a further note*] Antonio will be the guarantor. Well.

Bassanio   Will you oblige me? What's your decision?

Shylock   [*thinking*] Three thousand ducats for three months. And Antonio as guarantor . . .

Bassanio   So – your answer?

Shylock   Antonio is a good man.

Bassanio   Have you heard any imputation to the contrary?

Shylock   Oh no, no, no, no! My meaning in saying he is a good
15   man, is to have you understand me that he is sufficient. Yet
his means are in supposition: he hath an argosy bound to
Tripolis, another to the Indies; I understand moreover upon
the Rialto, he hath a third at Mexico, a fourth for England,
and other ventures he hath squandered abroad. But ships are
20   but boards, sailors but men – there be land-rats and water-
rats, land-thieves, and water-thieves, I mean pirates, and
then there is the peril of waters, winds, and rocks. The man
is, notwithstanding, sufficient. Three thousand ducats – I
think I may take his bond.

25 **Bassanio**   Be assured you may.

Shylock   I will be assured I may: and, that I may be assured, I
will bethink me. May I speak with Antonio?

Bassanio   If it please you to dine with us.

Shylock   Yes, to smell pork; to eat of the habitation which
30   your prophet the Nazarite conjured the devil into! I will buy
with you, sell with you, talk with you, walk with you, and so
following: but I will not eat with you, drink with you, nor
pray with you. What news on the Rialto? Who is he comes
here?

[*Enter* **Antonio**]

35 **Bassanio**   This is Signior Antonio.

Shylock   [*aside*]   How like a fawning publican he looks!
I hate him for he is a Christian:
But more for that in low simplicity
He lends out money gratis, and brings down

Shylock   Antonio is a good man . . .

Bassanio   Have you heard anything to the contrary?

Shylock   [*laughing*] Oh, no, no, no, no. When I say "a good man," you must understand that I mean he is financially sound. But his wealth is at risk. He has a merchant ship en route for Tripoli, and another is bound for the Indies. At the Rialto [merchants' exchange], I heard he has a third at Mexico, a fourth sailing for England, plus other foreign risks. But ships are only timbers. Sailors are only men. There are rats on land, and rats at sea. Thieves on land, and thieves at sea. Pirates, in other words. Then there's the danger of currents, storms and rocks. Nonetheless, the man is sound. Three thousand ducats. I think I can take his guarantee.

Bassanio   You certainly can!

Shylock   I *will* be certain I can. And to be certain, I'll think it over. May I speak with Antonio?

Bassanio   By all means. Have a meal with us.

Shylock   [*to himself*] Yes, to smell pork and eat the meat your Jesus turned into the devil! I'll buy from you, sell to you, talk with you, walk with you and so on – but I won't eat with you, or drink with you or pray with you. [*To* **Bassanio** *again*] What's the latest news from the Exchange? And who comes here?

[**Antonio** *enters*]

Bassanio   It's Antonio. [**Bassanio** *takes him to one side*]

Shylock   [*to himself*] How like a fawning innkeeper he looks! I hate him because he is a Christian. But worse because he humbly lends out money free of charge, bringing down the

40   The rate of usance here with us in Venice.
If I can catch him once upon the hip,
I will feed fat the ancient grudge I bear him.
He hates our sacred nation, and he rails,
Even there where merchants most do congregate,
45   On me, my bargains, and my well-won thrift,
Which he calls interest. Cursed be my tribe,
If I forgive him!

Bassanio   Shylock, do you hear?

Shylock I am debating of my present store,
50   And by the near guess of my memory
I cannot instantly raise up the gross
Of full three thousand ducats: What of that?
Tubal a wealthy Hebrew of my tribe
Will furnish me; but soft – how many months
55   Do you desire? [*To* **Antonio**] Rest you fair, good signior,
Your worship was the last man in our mouths.

Antonio Shylock, albeit I neither lend nor borrow
By taking nor by giving of excess,
Yet to supply the ripe wants of my friend
60   I'll break a custom. Is he yet possessed
How much ye would?

Shylock   Ay, ay, three thousand ducats.

Antonio And for three months.

Shylock I had forgot – three months – you told me so.
65   Well then, your bond: and let me see; but hear you,
Methought you said you neither lend nor borrow
Upon advantage.

Antonio   I do never use it.

Shylock When Jacob grazed his uncle Laban's sheep,
70   This Jacob from our holy Abram was,

rate of interest here in Venice. If I can catch him unawares, I'll pay off old scores very handsomely. He hates us Jews. In business circles, where the merchants meet, he denounces me, my deals and my hard-earned profit, which he calls "usury." May my tribe be cursed if I forgive him!

Bassanio [*sharply*] Shylock, are you listening?

Shylock I'm reckoning up my assets. At a rough guess, I don't think I can raise a full three thousand ducats. That's no matter. Tubal, a wealthy fellow-Hebrew, will fund me. But one moment. How many months do you want it for? [*He bows to* **Antonio**] Do not worry, sir. We were just speaking about you.

Antonio Shylock – though I never lend or borrow, by either receiving or demanding high returns, I'll make an exception to help my friend with his pressing needs. [*To* **Bassanio**] Does he know how much you want?

Shylock Oh, yes. Three thousand ducats.

Antonio And for three months.

Shylock I had forgotten. Yes, three months. You did tell me. Well, then. Your guarantee . . . let me see . . . [*he thinks*]. But listen. I thought you said you neither lend nor borrow for profit?

Antonio I never do.

Shylock When Jacob grazed his Uncle Laban's sheep – this Jacob was third in line of inheritance from Abraham, thanks to

As his wise mother wrought in his behalf,
The third possessor; ay, he was the third –

Antonio   And what of him? did he take interest?

Shylock   No, not take interest – not as you would say
75   Directly interest. Mark what Jacob did.
When Laban and himself were compromised
That all the eanlings which were streaked and pied
Should fall as Jacob's hire, the ewes, being rank
In end of autumn, turned to the rams,
80   And when the work of generation was
Between these woolly breeders in the act,
The skilful shepherd pilled me certain wands,
And, in the doing of the deed of kind,
He stuck them up before the fulsome ewes,
85   Who, then conceiving, did in eaning time
Fall parti-coloured lambs, and those were Jacob's.
This was a way to thrive, and he was blest:
And thrift is blessing if men steal it not.

Antonio   This was a venture, sir, that Jacob served for;
90   A thing not in his power to bring to pass,
But swayed and fashioned by the hand of heaven.
Was this inserted to make interest good?
Or is your gold and silver ewes and rams?

Shylock   I cannot tell, I make it breed as fast!
But note me, signior.

95 **Antonio**   Mark you this, Bassanio
The devil can cite Scripture for his purpose.
An evil soul, producing holy witness,
Is like a villain with a smiling cheek,
A goodly apple rotten at the heart.
100   O, what a goodly outside falsehood hath!

his mother's cunning [*he gets lost in theological thought*] — yes, he was the third . . .

Antonio   [*impatiently*] Yes, so what? Did he take interest?

Shylock   No. He didn't. Not what you would call *direct* interest. Note what Jacob did. When Laban and he were agreed that all the newborn lambs with stripes and markings should be his to keep as wages, the ewes (being in season) sought out the rams. And when these woolly animals were mating, the skillful shepherd peeled some sticks and stuck them up in sight of the lusty ewes. At this point they conceived. And so, at lambing time, they dropped lambs with mottled markings. These belonged to Jacob. This was a way to prosper, and in this he was blessed. Profit is blessed, provided men don't steal to get it.

Antonio   Jacob was involved in speculation, sir. The outcome wasn't in his hands. Heaven made the decision. [*He smiles at the Jew's lack of knowledge*] Did you tell us this to justify profit? Or are you saying your gold and silver are like ewes and rams?

Shylock   I can't say. But I make it breed as fast!

Antonio   Note this, Bassanio. When it suits his purpose, the Devil can quote the Scriptures. An evil man who quotes the Bible is like a villain with a smiling face or a rosy apple with a rotten center. Oh, how attractive falsehood can appear!

Shylock   Three thousand ducats: 'tis a good round sum.
Three months from twelve: then let me see the rate.

Antonio   Well, Shylock, shall we be beholding to you?

Shylock   Signior Antonio, many a time and oft
105   In the Rialto you have rated me
About my moneys and my usances:
Still have I borne it with a patient shrug,
For suff'rance is the badge of all our tribe.
You call me misbeliever, cut-throat dog,
110   And spit upon my Jewish gaberdine,
And all for use of that which is mine own.
Well then, it now appears you need my help:
Go to then, you come to me, and you say,
'Shylock, we would have moneys': you say so;
115   You that did void your rheum upon my beard,
And foot me as you spurn a stranger cur
Over your threshold. Moneys is your suit.
What should I say to you? Should I not say
'Hath a dog money? is it possible
120   A cur can lend three thousand ducats?' Or
Shall I bend low, and in a bondman's key,
With bated breath, and whisp'ring humbleness,
Say this:
'Fair sir, you spit on me on Wednesday last –
You spurned me such a day; another time
125   You called me dog; and for these courtesies
I'll lend you thus much moneys'?

Antonio   I am as like to call thee so again,
To spit on thee again, to spurn thee too!
If thou wilt lend this money, lend it not
130   As to thy friends – for when did friendship take
A breed for barren metal of his friend?
But lend it rather to thine enemy,

Shylock   Three thousand ducats! That's a good round sum. [*He consults his tables*] Three months out of twelve. Let me see the rate . . .

Antonio   Well, Shylock, shall we be obliged to you?

Shylock   Signior Antonio. Many a time on the Exchange you have berated me about my moneylending. I've always shrugged this off, patiently, because suffering is the trademark of our race. You call me an infidel, a cutthroat dog, and you spit on my Jewish garments. And all for using what belongs to me. Well, then. It seems you need my help. Right. You come to me, and you say, "Shylock, we'd like some money." That's what you say. You, who spat on my beard and kicked me as you would a strange dog out of your house. Money you want. What should I say to you? Shouldn't I say, "Has a dog money? Is it possible a mongrel can lend three thousand ducats?" Or shall I bow low, and like a servant, nervously, and in a small humble voice say this: "Oh, sir. You spat on me last Wednesday. You kicked me on such a day. Another time you called me 'dog.' So in return for these compliments, I'll lend you this much money?"

Antonio   I'll no doubt call you so again and spit on you and kick you, too! If you lend this money, don't lend it as if to your friends. What kind of friendship makes money from a friend?

Who if he break, thou mayst with better face
Exact the penalty.

Shylock   Why, look you, how you storm!
135   I would be friends with you and have your love,
Forget the shames that you have stained me with,
Supply your present wants, and take no doit
Of usance for my moneys, and you'll not hear me:
This is kind I offer.

Bassanio   This were kindness!

140 **Shylock**   This kindness will I show.
Go with me to a notary, seal me there
Your single bond, and, in a merry sport,
If you repay me not on such a day,
In such a place, such sum or sums as are
145   Expressed in the condition, let the forfeit
Be nominated for an equal pound
Of your fair flesh, to be cut off and taken
In what part of your body pleaseth me.

Antonio   Content, in faith – I'll seal to such a bond,
150   And say there is much kindness in the Jew.

Bassanio   You shall not seal to such a bond for me,
I'll rather dwell in my necessity.

Antonio   Why, fear not man, I will not forfeit it.
Within these two months, that's a month before
155   This bond expires, I do expect return
Of thrice three times the value of this bond.

Shylock   O father Abram! what these Christians are,
Whose own hard dealing teaches them suspect
The thoughts of others. Pray you, tell me this –
160   If he should break his day, what should I gain
By the exaction of the forfeiture?

Rather, lend it to your enemy. If he fails to pay, you can more decently impose the penalty.

Shylock Why, look how you storm! I want to be friends with you and have your love, forget your shameful treatment, provide the money you want, and take not a penny of interest! But you won't listen to me! I'm offering a kindness . . .

Bassanio Kindness indeed!

Shylock This is the kindness I'll show. Come with me to a solicitor. Sign your irrevocable bond, and – for fun – if you don't repay me on such a day, at such a place, such sum or sums as are in the contract, let the forfeit be agreed for a full pound of your fair flesh, to be cut off and taken from whatever part of your body I choose.

Antonio Certainly! I'll sign a bond like that, and say the Jew is showing considerable kindness.

Bassanio You mustn't sign such a bond for me. I'd rather manage without.

Antonio Oh, don't worry, man! I won't forfeit it. Within two months – that's a month before this bond expires – I'm expecting the return of nine times what the bond is worth.

Shylock Oh, Father Abraham! These Christians! Their own tough bargaining makes them distrust everybody. Please now, tell me this. If he should fail to pay, what would I gain by

A pound of man's flesh, taken from a man,
Is not so estimable, profitable neither,
As flesh of muttons, beefs, or goats. I say,
165   To buy his favour, I extend this friendship:
If he will take it, so; if not, adieu,
And, for my love, I pray you wrong me not.

Antonio   Yes, Shylock, I will seal unto this bond.

Shylock   Then meet me forthwith at the notary's,
170   Give him direction for this merry bond,
And I will go and purse the ducats straight,
See to my house left in the fearful guard
Of an unthrifty knave; and presently
I will be with you.

Antonio   Hie thee, gentle Jew!

[*Exit* **Shylock**]

175   The Hebrew will turn Christian – he grows kind.

Bassanio   I like not fair terms and a villain's mind.

Antonio   Come on – in this there can be no dismay,
My ships come home a month before the day.

[*Exeunt*]

insisting on the forfeit? A pound of human flesh, taken from a man, is not so saleable, or profitable, as the flesh of mutton, beef or goats. I'm saying that to buy his goodwill, I offer this friendship. If he'll take it – so. If not, goodbye. But don't put me in the wrong.

Antonio   Yes, Shylock. I'll sign the bond.

Shylock   Then meet me right away at the solicitor's. Give him instructions for this merry bond. I'll go and put the money together, and check the security of my house, which I've left in the unreliable hands of a wasteful wretch. [*He means his servant,* **Gobbo**] I'll join you soon.

Antonio   Farewell, gentle Jew!

[**Shylock** *enters his house*]

The Hebrew will turn Christian. He's getting kind.

Bassanio   I don't like square deals from crooked minds.

Antonio   Come on – there's no cause for anxiety. My ships are due home a month before settlement day.

[*They leave together, the deal agreed*]

53

Act two

Scene 1

Portia's house at Belmont. Enter the **Prince of Morocco,** *and three or four followers, with* **Portia, Nerissa,** *and their train.*

Morocco Mislike me not for my complexion,
 The shadowed livery of the burnished sun,
 To whom I am a neighbour and near bred.
 Bring me the fairest creature northward born,
5 Where Phoebus' fire scarce thaws the icicles,
 And let us make incision for your love,
 To prove whose blood is reddest, his or mine.
 I tell thee, lady, this aspect of mine
 Hath feared the valiant. By my love, I swear
10 The best-regarded virgins of our clime
 Have loved it too. I would not change this hue,
 Except to steal your thoughts, my gentle queen.

Portia In terms of choice I am not solely led
 By nice direction of a maiden's eyes:
15 Besides, the lott'ry of my destiny
 Bars me the right of voluntary choosing:
 But if my father had not scanted me
 And hedged me by his wit, to yield myself
 His wife who wins me by that means I told you,
20 Yourself, renowned prince, then stood as fair
 As any comer I have looked on yet
 For my affection.

Morocco   Even for that I thank you.
 Therefore, I pray you, lead me to the caskets
 To try my fortune. By this scimitar

Act two

Scene 1

Portia's house in Belmont. **The Prince of Morocco** *enters with his attendants, and* **Portia** *and* **Nerissa** *with their servants.*

Morocco   Do not dislike me because of my color. My dark skin is the uniform of those who live under the burning coppery sun. Bring me the handsomest man of the northern hemisphere, born where the sun is barely hot enough to melt icicles, and compare our love by cutting us. That would prove whose blood was reddest – his or mine. I tell you, lady: this face of mine has made brave men afraid. But, by my love, I swear the loveliest women of my region have loved it too. I would not change my color, gentle queen, except to win your love.

Portia   As far as choice is concerned, I don't go by looks. Besides, I'm denied the right to choose for myself, by the terms of a lottery. If my father hadn't restricted me in this way to marrying the winner, then you, famed Prince, would have stood as good a chance of gaining my love as any I have seen so far.

Morocco   I thank you for that. Therefore, please lead me to the caskets to try my fortune. By this sword – that has slain two

25   That slew the Sophy and a Persian prince
       That won three fields of Sultan Solyman
       I would o'erstare the sternest eyes that look:
       Outbrave the heart most daring on the earth:
       Pluck the young sucking cubs from the she-bear,
30   Yea, mock the lion when he roars for prey,
       To win thee, lady. But, alas the while!
       If Hercules and Lichas play at dice
       Which is the better man, the greater throw
       May turn by fortune from the weaker hand:
35   So is Alcides beaten by his page,
       And so may I, blind fortune leading me,
       Miss that which one unworthier may attain,
       And die with grieving.

Portia   You must take your chance,
       And either not attempt to choose at all,
40   Or swear, before you choose, if you choose wrong,
       Never to speak to lady afterward
       In way of marriage. Therefore be advised.

Morocco   Nor will not. Come, bring me unto my chance.

Portia   First, forward to the temple. After dinner
       Your hazard shall be made.

45 **Morocco**   Good fortune then!
       To make me blest or cursed'st among men.

Scene 2

Venice: a street. Enter **Lancelot Gobbo.**

Lancelot   Certainly my conscience will serve me to run from
this Jew my master. The fiend is at mine elbow, and tempts

mighty and famous warriors and won three battles against a Turkish Sultan – I'd outstare the sternest eyes that ever looked, be braver than the boldest man on earth, snatch from the mother bear her sucking cubs, yes, scorn the hunting lion, to win you, lady. But alas, if two champions roll at dice to decide who is the greater, luck may give the weaker one the highest score. Equally, a famous boxer could be beaten by his second. Being a hostage to fortune, I may lose what a lesser man may gain, and die with grief.

Portia   You must take that risk. You must either not attempt to choose at all, or promise, before you choose, that if you choose wrong, you will never propose marriage to a woman afterwards. Therefore, be cautious.

Morocco   Not me. To my chance, then!

Portia   First you must go to the temple to swear your vows. Your attempt shall be made after dinner.

Morocco   Here's hoping for luck! I'll be the happiest or most miserable of men!

Scene 2

In front of Shylock's house. His servant **Lancelot Gobbo** *enters, scratching his head and talking to himself.*

Lancelot   I can run away from my master the Jew with a clear conscience. The devil is behind me, tempting me, and saying:

me, saying to me, 'Gobbo, Lancelot Gobbo, good Lancelot,'
or 'good Gobbo,' or 'good Lancelot Gobbo, use your legs,
5   take the start, run away.' My conscience says, 'No; take heed
honest Lancelot, take heed honest Gobbo,' or as aforesaid,
'honest Lancelot Gobbo, do not run, scorn running with thy
heels.' Well, the most courageous fiend bids me pack. 'Via!'
says the fiend, 'away!' says the fiend, 'for the heavens, rouse
10   up a brave mind,' says the fiend, 'and run'. Well, my
conscience, hanging about the neck of my heart, says very
wisely to me: 'My honest friend, Lancelot, being an honest
man's son,' or rather an honest woman's son, for indeed my
father did something smack, something grow to; he had a
15   kind of taste; well, my conscience says, 'Lancelot, budge
not.' 'Budge,' says the fiend. 'Budge not,' says my
conscience. 'Conscience,' say I, 'you counsel well.'
'Fiend,' say I, 'you counsel well.' To be ruled by my
conscience, I should stay with the Jew my master, who, God
20   bless the mark, is a kind of devil; and to run away from the
Jew, I should be ruled by the fiend, who, saving your
reverence, is the devil himself. Certainly the Jew is the very
devil incarnation – and, in my conscience, my conscience is
but a kind of hard conscience, to offer to counsel me to stay
25   with the Jew. The fiend gives the more friendly counsel. I will
run, fiend. My heels are at your command: I will run.

[*Enter* **Old Gobbo,** *with a basket*]

Old Gobbo   Master young man, you, I pray you, which is the
way to Master Jew's?

Lancelot   O heavens, this is my true-begotten father, who
30   being more than sand-blind, high gravel-blind, knows me
not. I will try confusions with him.

Old Gobbo   Master, young gentleman, I pray you, which is
the way to Master Jew's?

"Gobbo, Lancelot Gobbo, good Lancelot," or "good Gobbo," or "Good Lancelot Gobbo. Use your legs. Get started. Run away." My conscience says: "No: beware, honest Lancelot; beware honest Gobbo," (or, as I said before, "honest Lancelot Gobbo"), "Do not run. Do not scamper." Well, the brave devil tells me to pack up. "Off you go," says the fiend. "Depart," says the fiend. "For heaven's sake, be brave," says the fiend, "and run!" Well, my conscience, like a weight on my heart, says very wisely to me: "My honest friend Lancelot, being an honest man's son" (or rather, an honest woman's son, because my father had a strong smell of dishonesty about him my conscience says: "Lancelot, don't budge!" "Budge," says the fiend. "Don't budge," says my conscience. "Conscience," I say, "you advise well." "Fiend," I say, "you advise well." To obey my conscience, I should stay with my master the Jew who (touch wood!) is a sort of devil. If I ran away from the Jew, I'd be obeying the fiend who (begging your pardon) is the devil himself. Certainly the Jew is the devil personified. Upon my word, my conscience is a tough sort of conscience, to suggest staying with the Jew. The fiend's advice is much more friendly. I will run, fiend. My heels are at your command. I'll run.

[*He runs and bumps into* **Old Gobbo,** *his father, who is blind and carrying a basket*]

Old Gobbo   Master young man, please, which is the way to Master Jew's?

Lancelot   [*aside*] Good heavens! this is my own true father! Being more than part-blind – almost stone-blind in fact – he doesn't recognize me. I'll tease him a bit.

Old Gobbo   Master young gentlemen, please, which is the way to Master Jew's?

Lancelot   Turn up on your right hand at the next turning, but,
35   at the next turning of all on your left; marry at the very next
turning turn of no hand, but turn down indirectly to the Jew's
house.

Old Gobbo   By God's sonties, 'twill be a hard way to hit. Can
you tell me whether one Lancelot that dwells with him, dwell
40   with him or no?

Lancelot   Talk you of young Master Lancelot? – [*aside*] Mark
me now, now will I raise the waters! Talk you of young Master
Lancelot?

Old Gobbo   No 'master', sir, but a poor man's son. His father,
45   though I say it, is an honest exceeding poor man, and God be
thanked, well to live.

Lancelot   Well, let his father be what a' will, we talk of young
Master Lancelot.

Old Gobbo   Your worship's friend and Lancelot, sir.

50 **Lancelot**   But I pray you, ergo, old man, ergo I beseech you,
talk you of young Master Lancelot?

Old Gobbo   Of Lancelot, an't please your mastership.

Lancelot   Ergo – Master Lancelot! Talk not of Master
Lancelot, father, for the young gentleman – according to fates
55   and destinies, and such old sayings, the sisters three, and such
branches of learning – is indeed deceased, or as you would say
in plain terms, gone to heaven.

Old Gobbo   Marry, God forbid! The boy was the very staff of
my age, my very prop.

60 **Lancelot**   Do I look like a cudgel or a hovel-post, a staff or a
prop? Do you know me, father?

Lancelot [*shouting in his ear, and speaking very rapidly*] Turn right at the next turning, but left at the next turning of all. At the very next turning, don't turn either way, but turn down indirectly to the Jew's house!

Old Gobbo   By all the saints, that's not going to be easy. Could you tell me whether a certain Lancelot, who lives with him, is living with him or not?

Lancelot   Are you referring to young Master Lancelot? [*Aside*] Watch this! A tearful bit coming up! [*To* **Old Gobbo**] Do you speak of young Master Lancelot?

Old Gobbo   Hardly, "master," sir. He's only a poor man's son. Though I say it myself, his father is a poor but exceedingly honest man, and, thank God, still living.

Lancelot   Well, whatever his father may be, here we talk of young Master Lancelot.

Old Gobbo   Just Lancelot . . .

Lancelot   But I ask you, therefore, old man, consider, I beg you, are you talking of young *Master* Lancelot?

Old Gobbo   Lancelot, with respect to your mastership.

Lancelot   Therefore, *Master* Lancelot! But don't talk of Master Lancelot, old man, for the young gentleman – according to Fates, Destinies, and similar old myths, the three Fatal Sisters and such branches of learning – is, indeed, deceased, or as you would say in plain terms, gone to heaven.

Old Gobbo   Oh, God forbid! The boy was the staff of my old age, a real prop.

Lancelot   [*deciding to reveal himself*] Do I look like a pole or a corner post, a staff or a prop? Do you know me, father?

Old Gobbo   Alack the day, I know you not, young gentleman, but I pray you tell me, is my boy – God rest his soul! – alive or dead?

65 **Lancelot**   Do you not know me, father?

Old Gobbo   Alack, sir, I am sand-blind, I know you not.

Lancelot   Nay, indeed, if you had your eyes, you might fail of the knowing me: it is a wise father that knows his own child. Well, old man, I will tell you news of your son. Give me your
70   blessing. Truth will come to light, murder cannot be hid long, a man's son may, but in the end truth will out.

Old Gobbo   Pray you, sir, stand up. I am sure you are not Lancelot, my boy.

Lancelot   Pray you let's have no more fooling about it, but
75   give me your blessing: I am Lancelot, your boy that was, your son that is, your child that shall be.

Old Gobbo   I cannot think you are my son.

Lancelot   I know not what I shall think of that: but I am Lancelot, the Jew's man, and I am sure Margery, your wife, is
80   my mother.

Old Gobbo   Her name is Margery, indeed. I'll be sworn, if thou be Lancelot, thou art mine own flesh and blood. Lord worshipped might he be! What a beard hast thou got! Thou hast got more hair on thy chin than Dobbin my fill-horse has
85   on his tail.

Lancelot   It should seem then that Dobbin's tail grows backward. I am sure he had more hair of his tail than I have of my face, when I last saw him.

Old Gobbo   Lord, how art thou changed! How dost thou and
90   thy master agree? I have brought him a present. How 'gree you now?

Old Gobbo Alas, I don't know you, young sir. But please tell me, is my boy (God rest his soul!) alive or dead?

Lancelot Don't you recognize me, father?

Old Gobbo Alas, sir, I'm almost blind. I don't recognize you.

Lancelot Even if you had your sight, you mightn't know me. It's a wise father that knows his own child. [*He kneels*] Well, old man, I'll give you news of your son. Give me your blessing. Truth will come to light, and murder cannot be long concealed, though a man's son may. In the end, truth will out.

Old Gobbo Please, sir. Stand up. I'm sure you aren't my boy, Lancelot.

Lancelot Let's have no more fooling about. Give me your blessing. I'm Lancelot. Your boy that was, your son that is, your child that shall be.

Old Gobbo I can't believe you are my son.

Lancelot There's no answer to that! But I am Lancelot, the Jew's man, and I'm certain Margery, your wife, is my mother.

Old Gobbo Her name is certainly Margery. So if you are Lancelot, I'll swear you are my own flesh and blood. [*He feels for* **Lancelot**'*s face, but* **Lancelot** *offers the back of his head*] Thank God! What a beard you've got! You've more hair on your chin than Dobbin my carthorse has on his tail!

Lancelot Dobbin's tail must grow backward, then. I'm sure he had more hair on his tail than I had on my face last time I saw him.

Old Gobbo Lord, how you've changed! How do you get along with your master? I've brought him a present. How do you get along?

Lancelot   Well, well: but, for mine own part, as I have set up
my rest to run away, so I will not rest till I have run some
ground. My master's a very Jew: give him a present! give him
95   a halter: I am famished in his service: you may tell every finger
I have with my ribs. Father, I am glad you are come. Give me
your present to one Master Bassanio, who indeed gives rare
new liveries. If I serve not him, I will run as far as God has any
ground. O rare fortune! here comes the man – to him, father,
100   for I am a Jew if I serve the Jew any longer.

[*Enter* **Bassanio** *with* **Leonardo** *and other followers*]

Bassanio   You may do so, but let it be so hasted that supper be
ready at the farthest by five of the clock. See these letters
delivered, put the liveries to making, and desire Gratiano to
come anon to my lodging.

[*Exit* **Servant**]

105   **Lancelot**   To him, father.

Old Gobbo   God bless your worship!

Bassanio   Gramercy! wouldst thou aught with me?

Old Gobbo   Here's my son, sir, a poor boy –

Lancelot   Not a poor boy, sir, but the rich Jew's man that
110   would, sir, as my father shall specify –

Old Gobbo   He hath a great infection, sir, as one would say to
serve –

Lancelot   Indeed the short and the long is, I serve the Jew, and
have a desire as my father shall specify –

115   **Old Gobbo**   His master and he, saving your worship's
reverence, are scarce cater-cousins –

Lancelot   Well enough. But speaking for myself, as I've made up my mind to run away, I won't rest until I've covered some ground. My master's a real Jew. Give him a present? Give him a noose! He starves me. My ribs feel like fingers. [*He stretches his fingers out over his chest and guides* **Old Gobbo***'s hand so that he can feel them*] Father, I'm glad you've come. Give the present to a certain Master Bassanio. He really does provide smart uniforms! Either I'll serve him or keep running. Oh, great! Here he comes. Go to him, father. If I serve the Jew any longer, despise me!

[*Enter* **Bassanio,** *with* **Leonardo** *and some friends*]

Bassanio   [*to a servant*] Yes, but be quick about it – supper at five at the latest. Deliver these letters. Order the servants' uniforms. Ask Gratiano to come to my house.

[*The* **Servant** *leaves*]

Lancelot   [*pushing his father forward*] Go to him, father!

Old Gobbo   [*bowing*] God bless your worship!

Bassanio   Thanks. Was there something?

Old Gobbo   Here's my son, sir, a poor boy –

Lancelot   [*coming forward*] Not a poor boy, sir, but the rich Jew's servant who would like, as my father will explain – [*he hides behind his father*]

Old Gobbo   He has a great ambition, sir, to (as they say) serve –

Lancelot   [*coming forward again*] Well, the short and the long of it is that I serve the Jew, but would like, as my father will explain – [*he retreats again*]

Old Gobbo   He and his master (with respect) are hardly on speaking terms.

Lancelot   To be brief, the very truth is, that the Jew having done me wrong, doth cause me as my father, being, I hope, an old man, shall frutify unto you –

120 **Old Gobbo**   I have here a dish of doves that I would bestow upon your worship, and my suit is –

Lancelot   In very brief, the suit is impertinent to myself, as your worship shall know by this honest old man, and though I say it, though old man, yet poor man, my father.

125 **Bassanio**   One speak for both. What would you?

Lancelot   Serve you, sir.

Old Gobbo   That is the very defect of the matter, sir.

Bassanio   I know thee well, thou hast obtained thy suit.
Shylock, thy master, spoke with me this day,
130   And hath preferred thee, if it be preferment
To leave a rich Jew's service, to become
The follower of so poor a gentleman.

Lancelot   The old proverb is very well parted between my master Shylock and you, sir. You have the grace of God, sir,
135   and he hath enough.

Bassanio   Thou speak'st it well; go, father, with thy son.
Take leave of thy old master, and inquire
My lodging out. Give him a livery
More guarded than his fellows': see it done.

140 **Lancelot**   Father, in. I cannot get a service, no! I have ne'er a tongue in my head! Well – if any man in Italy have a fairer table which doth offer to swear upon a book I shall have good fortune. Go to, here's a simple line of life, here's a small trifle of wives; alas, fifteen wives is nothing, eleven widows, and
145   nine maids, is a simple coming-in for one man; and then to scape drowning thrice, and to be in peril of my life with the

Lancelot [*appearing again*] In short, the plain truth is that the Jew, having wronged me, causes me, as my father (being, I hope, an old man) shall explain to you – [*back he goes once more*]

Bassanio   One can speak for both of you. [*To* **Lancelot**] What is it you want?

Lancelot   To serve you, sir.

Old Gobbo   That's the heart of the matter, sir.

Bassanio   I know you well. The job is yours. Shylock, your master, spoke to me today and recommended you – if it really is promotion to leave a rich Jew's service, to be the servant of a poor man like me.

Lancelot   The old proverb applies very well to you and my master Shylock, sir. You have God's grace, and he's got plenty of money.

Bassanio   Well put! Go, father, with your son. [*To* **Lancelot**] Say goodbye to your old master and go find my house. [*To his followers*] Give him a uniform that's fancier than the others. See it's done.

[*He talks aside with* **Leonardo**]

Lancelot   [*indicating* **Shylock**'s *house*] Father, after you. [*Mocking*] Oh, no – I can't get a servant's job! I can't speak up for myself! Well [*he pretends to read the palm of his hand*], did you ever see a palm more certain to give good fortune? Look at that life-line! And that small matter of wives! What's fifteen wives? Eleven widows and nine maidens is not much for this man. And then to escape drowning three times, and not get

edge of a feather-bed. Here are simple scapes. Well, if
Fortune be a woman, she's a good wench for this gear.
Father, come. I'll take my leave of the Jew in the twinkling of
150   an eye.

[*Exeunt* **Lancelot** *and* **Old Gobbo**]

Bassanio   I pray thee, good Leonardo, think on this:
These things being bought and orderly bestowed,
Return in haste, for I do feast tonight
My best-esteemed acquaintance. Hie thee, go.

155 **Leonardo**   My best endeavours shall be done herein.

[*Enter* **Gratiano**]

Gratiano   Where's your master?

Leonardo   Yonder, sir, he walks.

[*Exit* **Leonardo**]

Gratiano   Signior Bassanio!

Bassanio   Gratiano!

160 **Gratiano**   I have a suit to you.

Bassanio   You have obtained it.

Gratiano   You must not deny me. I must go with you to
Belmont.

Bassanio   Why, then you must. But hear thee Gratiano,
165   Thou art too wild, too rude, and bold of voice –
Parts that become thee happily enough,
And in such eyes as ours appear not faults;
But where thou art not known, why, there they show

caught when sleeping around – these are all minor escapades! If Fortune is a woman, she's the right girl for this work! Come on, father. I'll soon say farewell to the Jew.

[*They enter Shylock's house*]

Bassanio [*finishing his instructions*] Bear all this in mind, please, Leonardo. And when you've bought everything and sorted things out, come back quickly. I'm dining tonight with my best friend. Off you go.

Leonardo   I'll do my best.

[*As he leaves, he bumps into* **Gratiano**]

Gratiano   Where's your master?

Leonardo   Over there.

[*He leaves*]

Gratiano   Bassanio!

Bassanio   Gratiano!

Gratiano   I've a favor to ask.

Bassanio   Granted.

Gratiano   Don't say no. I want to go with you to Belmont.

Bassanio   Well then, do so. But listen, Gratiano. You are too wild, too rude, too outspoken: features which suit you well enough and seem all right to us. But among strangers, they

Something too liberal. Pray thee, take pain
170   To allay with some cold drops of modesty
Thy skipping spirit, lest through thy wild behaviour
I be misconstrued in the place I go to,
And lose my hopes.

Gratiano   Signior Bassanio, hear me:
175   If I do not put on a sober habit,
Talk with respect, and swear but now and then,
Wear prayer-books in my pocket, look demurely,
Nay more, while grace is saying, hood mine eyes
Thus with my hat, and sigh, and say 'amen';
180   Use all the observance of civility,
Like one well studied in a sad ostent
To please his grandam, never trust me more.

Bassanio   Well, we shall see your bearing.

Gratiano   Nay, but I bar tonight, you shall not gauge me
185   By what we do tonight.

Bassanio   No, that were pity,
I would entreat you rather to put on
Your boldest suit of mirth, for we have friends
That purpose merriment. But fare you well,
190   I have some business.

Gratiano   And I must to Lorenzo, and the rest.
But we will visit you at supper-time.

[*Exeunt*]

are a bit too much. Please try to moderate your high spirits. Try a little modesty. They could misunderstand me in Belmont. Your wild behavior might lose me my chances.

Gratiano   Bassanio, listen to me. If I don't dress soberly; talk respectfully; swear only now and again; carry prayerbooks in my pocket; look not only demure but, when they say grace, take my hat off, sigh and say "Amen"; be good-mannered always, like a man aiming to please his grandmother – never trust me again!

Bassanio   Well, we'll see how you act.

Gratiano   But tonight's an exception. You mustn't judge me by what we do tonight!

Bassanio   No, that would be a pity. I'd much rather you were at your funniest, for our friends intend to have a merry time. But goodbye for now, I have business to attend to.

Gratiano   And I must join Lorenzo, and the rest. See you at dinner!

[*They go their ways*]

Scene 3

Shylock's house. Enter **Jessica** *and* **Lancelot.**

Jessica   I am sorry thou wilt leave my father so.
Our house is hell, and thou, a merry devil,
Didst rob it of some taste of tediousness.
But fare thee well, there is a ducat for thee.
5   And, Lancelot, soon at supper shalt thou see
Lorenzo, who is thy new master's guest.
Give him this letter, do it secretly,
And so farewell: I would not have my father
See me in talk with thee.

10 **Lancelot**   Adieu! tears exhibit my tongue. Most beautiful
pagan, most sweet Jew! If a Christian did not play the knave
and get thee, I am much deceived. But adieu, these foolish
drops do something drown my manly spirit; adieu!

[*Exit*]

Jessica   Farewell, good Lancelot.
15   Alack, what heinous sin is it in me
To be ashamed to be my father's child!
But though I am a daughter to his blood,
I am not to his manners. O Lorenzo,
If thou keep promise, I shall end this strife,
20   Become a Christian, and thy loving wife.

[*Exit*]

Scene 3

Shylock's front door. **Jessica** *and* **Lancelot** *come out.*

Jessica   I'm sorry you are leaving my father like this. Our house is hell, and you – a merry devil – reduced the boredom. But goodbye – there's a ducat for you. And, Lancelot, around suppertime you'll see your new master's guest, Lorenzo. Give him this letter, secretly. And so, farewell. I don't want my father to see me talking to you.

Lancelot   Adieu! My tears speak for me. Most beautiful pagan! Most sweet Jewess! If a Christian didn't seduce your mother, I'm much mistaken. But goodbye! These foolish tears aren't manly. Goodbye!

[*He goes, drying his tears*]

Jessica   Farewell, good Lancelot. Alas, what a grievous sin it is in me to be ashamed to be my father's child! I may be a daughter of his blood, but I'm not related to his life-style. Oh, Lorenzo, if you keep your word, there'll be an end to all this conflict. I'll turn Christian and be your loving wife.

[*She goes indoors*]

Scene 4

Venice. A street. Enter **Gratiano, Lorenzo, Salerio** *and* **Solanio.**

Lorenzo Nay, we will slink away in supper-time,
Disguise us at my lodging, and return
All in an hour.

Gratiano We have not made good preparation.

5 **Salerio** We have not spoke as yet of torch-bearers.

Solanio 'Tis vile, unless it may be quaintly ordered,
And better in my mind not undertook.

Lorenzo 'Tis now but four o'clock: we have two hours
To furnish us.

[*Enter* **Lancelot**]

10   Friend Lancelot, what's the news?

Lancelot An it shall please you to break up this, it shall seem
to signify.

Lorenzo I know the hand. In faith 'tis a fair hand,
And whiter than the paper it writ on
Is the fair hand that writ.

15 **Gratiano**   Love-news, in faith.

Lancelot By your leave, sir.

Lorenzo Whither goest thou?

Lancelot Marry, sir, to bid my old master the Jew to sup
tonight with my new master the Christian.

Scene 4

Another street in Venice. Enter **Gratiano, Lorenzo, Salerio** *and* **Solanio,** *discussing preparations for their fancy-dress party.*

Lorenzo   No. We'll slink away at supper time, change our clothes at my lodgings and be back within the hour.

Gratiano   We haven't got things ready.

Salerio   We haven't hired torchbearers.

Solanio   It's stupid unless it's cleverly organized. I'd vote against it.

Lorenzo   It's not quite four o'clock. We have two hours to get things arranged.

  [*Enter* **Lancelot**]

What's the news, friend Lancelot?

Lancelot   [*producing a letter*] Open this and you'll know.

Lorenzo   I recognize the handwriting. It's neat, and the neat little hand that wrote it is whiter than the notepaper.

Gratiano   A love letter, by Jove!

Lancelot   Excuse me, sir. [*He is about to go*]

Lorenzo   Where are you off to?

Lancelot   Well, sir, to invite my old master, the Jew, to dine tonight with my new master, the Christian.

20 **Lorenzo**   Hold here, take this. Tell gentle Jessica
I will not fail her; speak it privately.

[*Exit* **Lancelot**]

Go, gentlemen,
Will you prepare you for this masque tonight?
I am provided of a torch-bearer.

25 **Salerio**   Ay, marry, I'll be gone about it straight.

Solanio   And so will I.

Lorenzo   Meet me and Gratiano
At Gratiano's lodging some hour hence.

Salerio   'Tis good we do so.

[*Exit* **Salerio** *and* **Solanio**]

Gratiano   Was not that letter from fair Jessica?

30 **Lorenzo**   I must needs tell thee all. She hath directed
How I shall take her from her father's house,
What gold and jewels she is furnished with,
What page's suit she hath in readiness.
If e'er the Jew her father come to heaven
35 It will be for his gentle daughter's sake,
And never dare misfortune cross her foot
Unless she do it under this excuse:
That she is issue to a faithless Jew.
Come, go with me. Peruse this, as thou goest.
40 Fair Jessica shall be my torch-bearer.

[*Exeunt*]

Lorenzo   Hold on. [*He gives him a tip*] For you. Tell dear Jessica I won't let her down. Tell her privately.

[**Lancelot** *leaves*]

Go, gentlemen. Get ready for tonight's masque [dramatic entertainment]. I've arranged my torchbearer.

Salerio   Right. I'll get started on it.

Solanio   So will I.

Lorenzo   Meet me and Gratiano at Gratiano's place in about an hour.

Salerio   A good idea.

[**Salerio** *and* **Solanio** *depart*]

Gratiano   Wasn't that letter from fair Jessica?

Lorenzo   I'd better tell you everything. She has told me how I shall take her from her father's house, what gold and jewels she will bring, and how she will dress as a page. If ever the Jew her father enters heaven, it will be on his daughter's account. May misfortune never cross her path, unless the excuse is that she's daughter to a Jew! Come with me. Read this as you go along. Jessica will be my torchbearer!

[*They walk off briskly*]

Scene 5

Outside Shylock's house. Enter **Shylock** *and* **Lancelot.**

Shylock Well, thou shalt see, thy eyes shall be by judge,
The difference of old Shylock and Bassanio –
What, Jessica! – Thou shalt not gormandize,
As thou hast done with me – What, Jessica! –
5   And sleep and snore, and rend apparel out –
Why, Jessica, I say!

Lancelot   Why, Jessica!

Shylock Who bids thee call? I do not bid thee call.

Lancelot Your worship was wont to tell me I could do nothing
without bidding.

[*Enter* **Jessica**]

10 **Jessica** Call you? What is your will?

Shylock I am bid forth to supper, Jessica.
There are my keys. But wherefore should I go?
I am not bid for love: they flatter me.
But yet I'll go in hate, to feed upon
15   The prodigal Christian. Jessica, my girl,
Look to my house. I am right loath to go:
There is some ill a-brewing towards my rest,
For I did dream of money-bags tonight.

Lancelot I beseech you, sir, go. My young master doth expect
20   your reproach.

Shylock So do I his.

Lancelot And they have conspired together. I will not say you
shall see a masque, but if you do, then it was not for nothing

Scene 5

Outside **Shylock's** *house.* **Shylock** *and* **Lancelot** *come out.*

Shylock   Well, you'll see! Your eyes will judge the difference between old Shylock and Bassanio. [*Calling*] Jessica! [*To* **Lancelot**] You won't stuff yourself as you have with me. [*Calling again*] What, Jessica! [*To* **Lancelot**] Or sleep and snore, and wear out your clothes. [*Calling louder*] What, Jessica, I say!

Lancelot [*helping*] Jessica!

Shylock   Who asked you to call? I didn't ask you to call.

Lancelot   Your worship used to say I never did anything without being asked.

[**Jessica** *appears*]

Jessica   Did you call? What is your wish?

Shylock   I'm invited out to dinner, Jessica. Here are my keys. But why should I go? I'm not invited out of love. They flatter me. But still, I'll go in hate, to eat the wasteful Christian's food. Jessica, my girl, look after my house. I'm loathe to go. Something's not right. I dreamed of moneybags last night.

Lancelot   I beg you to go, sir. My young master expects the displeasure of your company.

Shylock   As I do his.

Lancelot   And they've conspired together. I won't exactly say you'll see a masque, but [*winking*] if you do, it was not for

25 that my nose fell a-bleeding on Black-Monday last, at six
o'clock i'th' morning, falling out that year on
Ash-Wednesday was four year, in th'afternoon.

Shylock   What, are there masques? Hear you me, Jessica –
Lock up my doors, and when you hear the drum
And the vile squealing of the wry-necked fife,
30 Clamber not you up to the casements then,
Nor thrust your head into the public street
To gaze on Christian fools with varnished faces:
But stop my house's ears, I mean my casements,
Let not the sound of shallow fopp'ry enter
35 My sober house. By Jacob's staff I swear
I have no mind of feasting forth tonight:
But I will go. Go you before me, sirrah –
Say I will come.

Lancelot   I will go before, sir. [*Aside to* **Jessica**]
Mistress, look out
40 at window, for all this –

There will come a Christian by,
Will be worth a Jewess' eye.

[*Exit*]

Shylock   What says that fool of Hagar's offspring, ha?

Jessica   His words were, 'Farewell, mistress' – nothing else.

45 **Shylock**   The patch is kind enough, but a huge feeder,
Snail-slow in profit, and he sleeps by day
More than the wild-cat: drones hive not with me.
Therefore I part with him, and part with him
To one that I would have him help to waste
50 His borrowed purse. Well, Jessica, go in.
Perhaps I will return immediately.
Do as I bid you, shut doors after you.

nothing my nose bled on Black Monday, to mention but one weird coincidence among many.

Shylock   What, will there be masques? Listen to me, Jessica. Lock up my doors. And when you hear the drum and the wretched squealing of the fife player, don't rush off to the windows or stick your head out into the street to look at Christian idiots in painted masks. Plug my house's ears – close the shutters – and don't let the sound of mindless foolery enter my sober house. By Jacob's staff, I swear I have no wish to dine out tonight. But I'll go. [*To* **Lancelot**] Go ahead, you. Say I'll come.

Lancelot   I'll go ahead, sir. [*As he departs, he whispers to* **Jessica**] Miss – look out of the windows because [*reciting*]

A certain Christian will come by
Worth the sight of a Jewess's eye.

[*He leaves whistling*]

Shylock   What did that idiot Gentile say?

Jessica   He said, "Farewell, mistress." Nothing else.

Shylock   The fool is kind enough, but a huge eater, a snail-slow worker, and he sleeps more during the day than a wildcat. I'll have no lazy ones in my house, therefore I let him go – to someone whom he can help waste borrowed money. Well, Jessica, in you go. I may return immediately. Do as I tell you,

> Fast bind, fast find,
> A proverb never stale in thrifty mind.

[Exit]

55 **Jessica**   Farewell – and if my fortune be not crost,
I have a father, you a daughter, lost.

[Exit]

Scene 6

Another street in Venice. Enter **Gratiano** *and* **Salerio**.

Gratiano   This is the pent-house, under which Lorenzo
Desired us to make stand.

Salerio   His hour is almost past.

Gratiano   And it is marvel he out-dwells his hour,
For lovers ever run before the clock.

5 **Salerio**   O, ten times faster Venus' pigeons fly
To seal love's bonds new-made, than they are wont
To keep obliged faith unforfeited!

Gratiano   That ever holds: who riseth from a feast
With that keen appetite that he sits down?
10 Where is the horse that doth untread again
His tedious measures with the unbated fire
That he did pace them first? All things that are,
Are with more spirit chased than enjoyed.
How like a younger or a prodigal
15 The scarfed bark puts from her native bay,

and shut doors behind you. "Lock tight, and all's right" – a proverb ever fresh to a thrifty mind. [*He goes*]

Jessica   Farewell. If all goes well, I've lost a father, and you've lost a daughter. [*She goes inside*]

Scene 6

A street. **Gratiano** *and* **Salerio** *appear, masked.*

Gratiano   This is the porch under which Lorenzo asked us to wait.

Salerio   He's late.

Gratiano   Strange he's overdue. Lovers are usually early.

Salerio   They're ten times faster in pursuit of love than in defense of constancy!

Gratiano   It's always the same. Who rises from dinner as hungry as he sat down? When does a horse return as briskly as it set out? In every way, the chase is more enjoyable than the catch. How like a carefree teenager a garland ship leaves her home port, riding the unbridled wind and loving it.

Hugged and embraced by the strumpet wind!
How like the prodigal doth she return,
With over-weathered ribs and ragged sails,
Lean, rent, and beggared by the strumpet wind!

[*Enter* **Lorenzo**]

20 **Salerio**   Here comes Lorenzo – more of this hereafter.

Lorenzo   Sweet friends, your patience for my long abode.
Not I, but my affairs, have made you wait:
When you shall please to play the thieves for wives
I'll watch as long for you then. Approach
25 Here dwells my father Jew. Ho! who's within?

[*Enter* **Jessica** *above, at a window*]

Jessica   Who are you? Tell me, for more certainty,
Albeit I'll swear that I do know your tongue.

Lorenzo   Lorenzo, and thy love.

Jessica   Lorenzo, certain, and my love indeed,
30 For who love I so much? And now who knows
But you, Lorenzo, whether I am yours?

Lorenzo   Heaven and thy thoughts are witness that thou art.

Jessica   Here, catch this casket, it is worth the pains.
I am glad 'tis night, you do not look on me,
35 For I am much ashamed of my exchange:
But love is blind, and lovers cannot see
The pretty follies that themselves commit,
For if they could, Cupid himself would blush
To see me thus transformed to a boy.

40 **Lorenzo**   Descend, for you must be my torch-bearer.

But how like a prodigal son it comes back home —
weatherbeaten, sails all torn, thin, leaky, and ruined by its
buffeting!

[**Lorenzo** *approaches in haste*]

Salerio   Here's Lorenzo. More about this later!

Lorenzo   Good friends: forgive my lateness. It was business,
not myself, that kept you waiting. When you take up wife-
stealing, I'll do the same for you. Come. Here is where my
Jewish father lives. [*He calls*] Hello! Anybody at home!

[*A window opens, and* **Jessica** *appears, dressed as a boy*]

Jessica   [*peering into the darkness*] Who's that? Although I
think I know your voice, say who you are!

Lorenzo   Lorenzo, and your love!

Jessica   Lorenzo certainly, and my love for sure! Whom do I
love so much? Only you, Lorenzo, can say whether I am yours.

Lorenzo   Heaven and your thoughts are witness that you are!

Jessica   Here. Catch this casket. It is worth the trouble. [*She
throws it down*] I'm glad it's night and you can't see me. I'm
shy about my clothes. But love is blind, and lovers cannot see
their foolishness. If they could, Cupid would blush to see me
changed into a boy.

Lorenzo   Come down. You must be my torchbearer.

Jessica   What, must I hold a candle to my shames?
They in themselves, good sooth, are too too light.
Why, 'tis an office of discovery, love,
And I should be obscured.

Lorenzo   So are you, sweet,
45   Even in the lovely garnish of a boy.
But come at once,
For the close night doth play the runaway,
And we are stayed for at Bassanio's feast.

Jessica   I will make fast the doors, and gild myself
50   With some more ducats, and be with you straight.

[*She closes the casement*]

Gratiano   Now, by my hood, a gentle and no Jew.

Lorenzo   Beshrew me but I love her heartily,
For she is wise, if I can judge of her,
And fair she is, if that mine eyes be true,
55   And true she is, as she hath proved herself:
And therefore, like herself, wise, fair, and true,
Shall she be placed in my constant soul.

[*Enter* **Jessica**]

What, art thou come? On, gentlemen, away!
60   Our masquing mates by this time for us stay.

[*Exeunt*]

[*Enter* **Antonio**]

Antonio   Who's there?

Gratiano   Signior Antonio!

Jessica   What, must my shame be so lit up? Indeed, it shines out quite enough the way it is. Love abides in modesty, and I should be concealed.

Lorenzo   And so you are, darling, being in the fetching disguise of a boy. But come at once. Night is passing quickly, and they are expecting us at Bassanio's party.

Jessica   I'll lock the doors, load up with more money, and be down straight away.

[*She closes the window*]

Gratiano   She's more a Gentile than a Jew!

Lorenzo   By heaven, I love her dearly! If I'm any judge, she's wise, and if my eyes tell true, she's beautiful. That she's faithful, she has just proved. Therefore her image – wise, beautiful and faithful – resides within my constant soul.

[**Jessica** *comes from the house*]

You are here, then. Come on, gentlemen! Let's away. Our companions in the masque are waiting for us.

[*He departs with* **Jessica** *and* **Salerio**]

[**Antonio** *comes walking down the street*]

Antonio   Who's there?

Gratiano   [*peering in the darkness*] Is that Signior Antonio?

Antonio   Fie, fie, Gratiano! where are all the rest?
'Tis nine o'clock; our friends all stay for you.
65   No masque tonight, the wind is come about,
Bassanio presently will go aboard.
I have sent twenty out to seek for you.

Gratiano   I am glad on't. I desire no more delight
Than to be under sail and gone tonight.

[*Exeunt*]

Scene 7

Portia's house at Belmont. Enter **Portia**, *with the* **Prince of Morocco**, *and their trains.*

Portia   Go, draw aside the curtains, and discover
The several caskets to this noble prince.
Now make your choice.

Morocco   The first, of gold, who this inscription bears:
5   'Who chooseth me shall gain what many men desire'.
The second, silver, which this promise carries:
'Who chooseth me shall get as much as he deserves'.
The third, dull lead, with warning all as blunt:
'Who chooseth me must give and hazard all he hath'.
10   How shall I know if I do choose the right?

Portia   The one of them contains my picture, prince.
If you choose that, then I am yours withal.

Morocco   Some god direct my judgement! Let me see,
I will survey th'inscriptions back again.
15   What says this leaden casket?

Antonio   Shame on you, Gratiano! Where is everybody? It's nine o'clock, and our friends are waiting for you. The masque is off. There's a fair wind, and Bassanio is ready to embark. I've sent twenty men out to look for you.

Gratiano   That suits me. I want nothing better than to be under sail and on my way tonight.

[*They leave hurriedly*]

Scene 7

The hall of Portia's house in Belmont. **Portia** *enters, with the* **Prince of Morocco** *and their* **Servants** *and* **Attendants**.

Portia [*to* **Servant**] Go and draw aside the curtains, to show the noble Prince the various caskets. [*The curtains are drawn back. Three caskets are displayed on a table*] Now make your choice.

[*The* **Prince** *examines each one in turn*]

Morocco   The first, of gold, bears this inscription: ''Who chooses me shall gain what many men desire.'' The second, of silver, carries this promise: ''Who chooses me shall get as much as he deserves.'' The third, made of dull lead, has a warning just as blunt: ''Who chooses me must give and gamble all he has.'' How shall I know if I have chosen the right one?

Portia   One of them contains my picture, Prince. If you choose that one, then I am yours.

Morocco   May some god guide my judgment! Let me see. I'll review the inscriptions over again. What does the lead casket

'Who chooseth me must give and hazard all he hath.'
Must give: for what? for lead? hazard for lead?
This casket threatens. Men that hazard all
Do it in hope of fair advantages:
20 A golden mind stoops not to shows of dross.
I'll then nor give nor hazard aught for lead.
What says the silver with her virgin hue?
'Who chooseth me shall get as much as he deserves.'
As much as he deserves! Pause there, Morocco,
25 And weigh thy value with an even hand.
If thou be'st rated by thy estimation,
Thou dost deserve enough – and yet enough
May not extend so far as to the lady:
And yet to be afeard of my deserving
30 Were but a weak disabling of myself.
As much as I deserve! Why, that's the lady.
I do in birth deserve her, and in fortunes,
In graces, and in qualities of breeding:
But more than these, in love I do deserve.
35 What if I strayed no further, but chose here?
Let's see once more this saying graved in gold:
'Who chooseth me shall gain what many men desire.'
Why, that's the lady – all the world desires her;
From the four corners of the earth they come,
40 To kiss this shrine, this mortal-breathing saint.
The Hyrcanian deserts and the vasty wilds
Of wide Arabia are as throughfares now
For princes to come view fair Portia.
The watery kingdom, whose ambitious head
45 Spits in the face of heaven, is no bar
To stop the foreign spirits, but they come,
As o'er a brook, to see fair Portia.
One of these three contains her heavenly picture.
Is't like that lead contains her? 'Twere damnation
50 To think so base a thought – it were too gross

say? "Who chooses me shall give and gamble all he has."
Must give? For what? For lead? Risk all for lead? This casket
looks dangerous. Men who risk all, do so hoping for good
returns. A mind of golden qualities does not stoop to tawdry
displays. Therefore I won't give or gamble anything for lead!
What says the silver with its virginal color? "Who chooses me
shall get as much as he deserves." As much as he deserves?
Pause there, Morocco, and weigh up your value even-
handedly. Valued by your own esteem, you do deserve
enough. But enough may not stretch as far as to the lady. Yet,
to be afraid of my own worthiness would be to underestimate
myself. As much as I deserve! Why, that's the lady! In terms of
birth I deserve her, and in fortune, manners and qualities of
breeding. Above all else, I deserve her in love. What if I went
no further, but chose here? Let's see once more the saying
engraved on the gold. "Who chooses me shall gain what
many men desire." Why, that's the lady—all the world desires
her. From the four corners of the earth they come, to kiss this
saint among mortals. The wildest deserts and those of vast
Arabia are highways now for princes who come to see fair
Portia. One of these three caskets contains her divine picture.
Is it likely that lead would contain her? It's damnable to think

To rib her cerecloth in the obscure grave.
Or shall I think in silver she's immured,
Being ten times undervalued to tried gold?
O sinful thought! Never so rich a gem
55   Was set in worse than gold. They have in England
A coin that bears the figure of an angel
Stamped in gold, but that's insculped upon;
But here an angel in a golden bed
Lies all within. Deliver me the key:
60   Here do I choose, and thrive I as I may!

Portia   There, take it, prince, and if my form lie there,
Then I am yours.

[*He unlocks the golden casket*]

Morocco   O hell! what have we here?
A carrion Death, within whose empty eye
There is a written scroll! I'll read the writing.

65   'All that glisters is not gold,
Often have you heard that told.
Many a man his life hath sold,
But my outside to behold.
Gilded tombs do worms infold.
70   Had you been as wise as bold,
Young in limbs, in judgement old,
Your answer had not been inscrolled –
Fare you well, your suit is cold.'

Cold, indeed, and labour lost.
75   Then, farewell heat, and welcome frost.
Portia, adieu! I have too grieved a heart
To take a tedious leave: thus losers part.

[*Exit with his train*]

so base a thought, and unthinkable to imagine her so
wrapped, as if for burial. Or shall I imagine her entombed in
silver, which is ten times less valuable than true gold? A sinful
thought! No gem so rich was ever set in anything less than
gold. In England they have a gold coin called an Angel, with
the image of an angel stamped on it. It's only engraved. But
inside here an angel lies upon a golden bed. Give me the key. I
choose this one, and take my chance!

Portia   [*handing over the key*] There, take it, Prince, and if my
picture is inside, then I am yours.

[*He unlocks the golden casket*]

Morocco   O hell! what have we here? A rotting skull, and in
its empty eye socket there's a rolled-up manuscript. I'll read
the writing on it:

> All that glitters is not gold;
> Often have you heard that told.
> Many a man his life has sold
> Just my outside to behold.
> Golden tombs do worms enfold.
> Had you been as wise as bold,
> Young in limbs, in wisdom old,
> Your answer would not be enscrolled –
> Fare you well. Your suit is cold.

Cold indeed, and labor lost.
So – farewell heat, and welcome frost.
Portia, goodbye! My heart is too grieved for a lengthy
farewell. [*Bowing*] Thus losers depart.

[*He leaves with his **Attendants**]

Portia   A gentle riddance. Draw the curtains, go.
Let all of his complexion choose me so.

[*Exeunt*]

Scene 8

A street in Venice. Enter **Salerio** *and* **Solanio.**

Salerio   Why man, I saw Bassanio under sail,
With him is Gratiano gone along:
And in their ship I am sure Lorenzo is not.

Solanio   The villain Jew with outcries raised the duke,
5   Who went with him to search Bassanio's ship.

Salerio   He came too late, the ship was under sail,
But there the duke was given to understand
That in a gondola were seen together
Lorenzo and his amorous Jessica.
10   Besides, Antonio certified the duke
They were not with Bassanio in his ship.

Solanio   I never heard a passion so confused,
So strange, outrageous, and so variable,
As the dog Jew did utter in the streets.
15   'My daughter! O my ducats! O my daughter!
Fled with a Christian! O my Christian ducats!
Justice! the law! my ducats, and my daughter!
A sealed bag, two sealed bags of ducats,
Of double ducats, stol'n from me by my daughter!
20   And jewels – two stones, two rich and precious stones,
Stol'n by my daughter! Justice! find the girl!
She hath the stones upon her, and the ducats!'

Portia   Good riddance! [*To the* **Servants**] Draw the curtains. May all with his vain disposition choose the same!

[*They exit*]

Scene 8

A street in Venice. Enter **Salerio** *and* **Solanio**.

Salerio   Why, man, I saw Bassanio set sail. Gratiano has gone along with him. I'm sure Lorenzo isn't on board.

Solanio   The villainous Jew's outcries roused the duke, who went with him to search Bassanio's ship.

Salerio   He arrived too late. The ship was under way. But the duke was informed that Lorenzo and his lovelorn Jessica were seen together in a gondola. Besides, Antonio certified to the duke that they were not with Bassanio in his ship.

Solanio   I've never heard an outcry so confused, so strange, so outrageous, and so inconsistent, as that of the dog Jew in the public street [*he impersonates the distressed* **Shylock**]: "My daughter! Oh, my ducats! Oh, my daughter! Fled with a Christian! Oh, my Christian money! Justice! The law! My ducats, and my daughter! A sealed bag, two sealed bags of money – golden ducats – stolen from me by my daughter! And jewels – two stones, two rich and precious stones, stolen by my daughter! Justice! Find the girl! She has the stones upon her, and the money!"

Salerio   Why, all the boys in Venice follow him,
Crying, his stones, his daughter, and his ducats.

25 **Solanio**   Let good Antonio look he keep his day,
Or he shall pay for this.

Salerio   Marry, well remembered:
I reasoned with a Frenchman yesterday,
Who told me, in the narrow seas that part
The French and English, there miscarried
30   A vessel of our country richly fraught:
I thought upon Antonio when he told me,
And wished in silence that it were not his.

Solanio   You were best to tell Antonio what you hear –
Yet do not suddenly, for it may grieve him.

35 **Salerio**   A kinder gentleman treads not the earth.
I saw Bassanio and Antonio part.
Bassanio told him he would make some speed
Of his return: he answered, 'Do not so.
Slubber not business for my sake, Bassanio,
40   But stay the very riping of the time.
And for the Jew's bond which he hath of me,
Let it not enter in your mind of love:
Be merry, and employ your chiefest thoughts
To courtship, and such fair ostents of love
45   As shall conveniently become you there.'
And even there, his eye being big with tears,
Turning his face, he put his hand behind him,
And with affection wondrous sensible
He wrung Bassanio's hand, and so they parted.

50 **Solanio**   I think he only loves the world for him.
I pray thee, let us go and find him out,
And quicken his embraced heaviness
With some delight or other.

Salerio [*laughing*] Why, all the boys in Venice follow him, crying "His stones! His daughter! His money!"

Solanio [*serious now*] Antonio had better settle up on time, or he will pay for this.

Salerio Indeed yes – well remembered. I chatted with a Frenchman yesterday, who told me that a rich Venetian ship had foundered in the English Channel. I thought about Antonio when he told me, and silently hoped it was not his.

Solanio You'd better tell Antonio what you heard. Do it gently. It may grieve him.

Salerio There's no kinder man on earth. I saw Bassanio and Antonio part. Bassanio said he'd return as soon as possible. "You mustn't. Don't skimp the business for my sake, Bassanio, but stay till the time is ripe. As for the Jew's bond, don't let it affect your love plans. Be cheerful and concentrate on courtship, and such demonstrations of love that seem appropriate there." And at this point his eyes filled with tears, and turning his face away, he stretched out his hand behind him. With astonishing, profound affection, he shook Bassanio's hand. And so they parted.

Solanio I think he means the world to him. Right, then, let's go and find him and try to snap him out of his low spirits with some amusement or other.

Salerio   Do we so.

                                             [*Exeunt*]

Scene 9

Portia's house at Belmont. Enter **Nerissa** *and a* **Servitor.**

Nerissa   Quick, quick, I pray thee – draw the curtain straight.
    The Prince of Arragon hath ta'en his oath,
    And comes to his election presently.

[*Enter* **Portia** *with the* **Prince of Arragon,** *and their trains*]

Portia   Behold, there stand the caskets, noble prince.
5   If you choose that wherein I am contained,
    Straight shall our nuptial rites be solemnized:
    But if you fail, without more speech, my lord,
    You must be gone from hence immediately.

Arragon   I am enjoined by oath to observe three things:
10   First, never to unfold to any one
    Which casket 'twas I chose; next, if I fail
    Of the right casket, never in my life
    To woo a maid in way of marriage;
        Lastly,
    If I do fail in fortune of my choice,
15   Immediately to leave you and be gone.

Portia   To these injunctions every one doth swear
    That comes to hazard for my worthless self.

Arragon   And so have I addressed me. Fortune now
    To my heart's hope! Gold, silver, and base lead.

Salerio Let's do that.

[*They move on*]

Scene 9

Portia*'s house at Belmont. The casket room. A* **Servant** *stands on guard.* **Nerissa** *runs in.*

Nerissa Quick, quick! Please draw the curtains right away! The Prince of Arragon has sworn his oath, and he's coming to make his choice immediately.

[*The* **Servant** *draws the curtains aside*]

[**Portia** *enters with the* **Prince of Arragon,** *a pompous man, and their* **Attendants**]

Portia Look – there stand the caskets, noble Prince. If you choose the one my picture's in, we'll be married straight away. But if you fail, you must say nothing, my lord, and leave here immediately.

Arragon I'm bound by oath to observe three things. First, never to disclose to anyone which casket it was that I chose. Second, if I fail to choose the right casket, never in my life will I woo a woman with a view to marriage. Lastly, if I'm unlucky in my choice, to leave you at once and depart.

Portia These are the conditions everyone must swear to who comes to gamble for my worthless self.

Arragon And I have weighed all this. May fortune grant me my heart's desire! [*He considers the caskets*] Gold, silver and

20   'Who chooseth me must give and hazard all he hath.'
You shall look fairer, ere I give or hazard.
What says the golden chest? ha! let me see:
'Who chooseth me shall gain what many men desire.'
What many men desire! that 'many' may be meant
25   By the fool multitude that choose by show,
Not learning more than the fond eye doth teach;
Which pries not to th'interior, but, like the martlet,
Builds in the weather on the outward wall,
Even in the force and road of casualty.
30   I will not choose what many men desire,
Because I will not jump with common spirits,
And rank me with the barbarous multitudes.
Why, then to thee, thou silver treasure-house!
Tell me once more what title thou dost bear:
35   'Who chooseth me shall get as much as he deserves.'
And well said too; for who shall go about
To cozen fortune and be honourable
Without the stamp of merit? Let none presume
To wear an undeserved dignity.
40   O, that estates, degrees and offices,
Were not derived corruptly, and that clear honour
Were purchased by the merit of the wearer!
How many then should cover that stand bare!
How many be commanded that command!
45   How much low peasantry would then be gleaned
From the true seed of honour! and how much honour
Picked from the chaff and ruin of the times,
To be new varnished! Well, but to my choice.
'Who chooseth me shall get as much as he deserves.'
50   I will assume desert. Give me a key for this –
And instantly unlock my fortunes here.

[*He opens the casket*]

base lead. "Who chooses me must give and risk all he has."
You must be prettier before I'll give or risk. What does the gold
chest say? Ah, let me see. "Who chooses me shall gain what
many men desire." What many men desire! By that "many"
may be meant the idiot majority who choose by outward
show, judging by the eye alone. They don't go into things
deeply, but act like those birds which build nests on outer
walls, at the mercy of the weather, right in the way of danger. I
will not choose what many men desire. I don't share common
tastes or count myself one of the ignorant masses. Well, then,
to you, the silver treasure house! Tell me again what
inscription you carry. "Who chooses me shall get as much
as he deserves." And well said, too! For who goes fortune-
hunting, seeking honor, without due merit? Nobody should
assume a status he doesn't deserve! Would that lands, titles
and public offices were never gained corruptly, and that
honors were always earned by merit! How many men would
keep their hats on instead of raising them politely? How many
would be bossed, instead of bossing? How many laborers
would be recruited from the ranks of the nobility, and how
many new nobles would be promoted from the castoffs and
dropouts of society! Be that as it may: to my choice. "Who
chooses me shall get as much as he deserves." [*He picks up
the silver casket*] Give me the key for this one, and unlock my
fortunes without dela⟩. [*He opens the casket and stands back,
shocked*]

Portia   Too long a pause for that which you find there.

Arragon   What's here? the portrait of a blinking idiot
Presenting me a schedule! I will read it.
How much unlike art thou to Portia!
55   How much unlike my hopes and my deservings!
'Who chooseth me shall have as much as he deserves.'
Did I deserve no more than a fool's head?
Is that my prize? are my deserts no better?

60 **Portia**   To offend and judge are distinct offices,
And of opposed natures.

Arragon   What is here?

'The fire seven times tried this:
Seven times tried that judgement is
That did never choose amiss.
65   Some there be that shadows kiss;
Such have but a shadow's bliss;
There be fools alive, I wis,
Silvered o'er – and so was this.
Take what wife you will to bed,
70   I will ever be your head:
So be gone, you are sped.'

Still more fool I shall appear
By the time I linger here.
With one fool's head I came to woo,
75   But I go away with two.
Sweet, adieu! I'll keep my oath,
Patiently to bear my ruth.

[*He exits with his train*]

Portia   Thus hath the candle singed the moth:
O, these deliberate fools! when they do choose,
80   They have the wisdom by their wit to lose.

Portia You've paused too long for what you find there.

Arragon What's here? The portrait of a gibbering idiot, offering me a note. I'll read it. [*Shuddering at the picture*] How unlike you are to Portia! How very different were my hopes and my deservings! "Who chooses me shall have as much as he deserves." Did I deserve nothing better than a clown's head? Is that my prize? Do I deserve no better?

Portia To offend is one thing and to judge another. They are opposite functions.

Arragon [*opening the document*] What's here?

Seven times through fire has this
Been tried – as every judgment is
That never once did choose amiss.
Some there are whom shadows kiss,
Some have but a shadow's bliss;
There are fools alive, I'd say,
Who are ensilvered in this way.
It matters not which wife you wed
I will always be your head
So be off, for you are sped.

The more the fool I will appear
By stretching out the time I'm here.
With one fool's head I came to woo
I go away, and wearing two.
Sweet, farewell! My word I'll keep:
With patience bear my sorrows deep.

[*He departs with his* **Attendants**]

Portia [*relieved*] Another moth singed by a tempting candle! Oh, these pompous fools! When they choose, they're so clever they get things wrong!

Nerissa   The ancient saying is no heresy,
  Hanging and wiving goes by destiny.

Portia   Come, draw the curtain, Nerissa.

[*Enter a* **Servant**]

Servant   Where is my lady?

Portia   Here – what would my lord?

85 **Servant**   Madam, there is alighted at your gate
  A young Venetian, one that comes before
  To signify th'approaching of his lord,
  From whom he bringeth sensible regreets:
  To wit, besides commends and courteous breath,
90   Gifts of rich value. Yet I have not seen
  So likely an ambassador of love.
  A day in April never came so sweet,
  To show how costly summer was at hand,
  As this fore-spurrer comes before his lord.

95 **Portia**   No more, I pray thee. I am half afeard,
  Thou wilt say anon he is some kin to thee,
  Thou spend'st such high-day wit in praising him.
  Come, come, Nerissa, for I long to see
  Quick Cupid's post that comes so mannerly.

100 **Nerissa**   Bassanio, lord Love, if thy will it be!

                                        [*Exeunt*]

Nerissa   The old saying got it right. ''To hang or to marry is a matter of Fate.''

Portia   Come, draw the curtain, Nerissa.

[*She does so. A* **Servant** *enters*]

Servant   [*to* **Nerissa**] Where is my lady?

Portia   I'm here. [*In high spirits*] What is it?

Servant   Madam, a young Venetian [*it is, of course,* **Gratiano**] has arrived at your door ahead of his master to announce his arrival. He has brought substantial offerings: that is to say, apart from recommendations and compliments, gifts of great value. Until now I haven't seen so promisng an ambassador on behalf of love. No sweet April day ever anticipated the approach of summer better than this forerunner does his master.

Portia   Say no more! I'm half afraid you'll say he's some relative of yours, you praise him so eloquently. Come, come, Nerissa. I long to see this messenger of Cupid who seems so gentle.

Nerissa   May it be Bassanio, Lord of Love willing!

[*Everyone goes out*]

Act three

Scene 1

A street in Venice. Enter **Solanio** *and* **Salerio** *meeting.*

Solanio Now, what news on the Rialto?

Salerio Why, yet it lives there unchecked that Antonio hath a
ship of rich lading wrecked on the narrow seas; the Goodwins,
I think they call the place; a very dangerous flat and fatal,
5 where the carcases of many a tall ship lie buried, as they say, if
my gossip Report be an honest woman of her word.

Solanio I would she were as lying a gossip in that, as ever
knapped ginger, or made her neighbours believe she wept for
the death of a third husband. But it is true, without any slips
10 of prolixity or crossing the plain highway of talk, that the
good Antonio, the honest Antonio – O, that I had a title good
enough to keep his name company –

Salerio Come, the full stop.

Solanio Ha! what sayest thou? Why, the end is, he hath lost a
15 ship.

Salerio I would it might prove the end of his losses.

Solanio Let me say 'amen' betimes, lest the devil cross my
prayer, for here he comes in the likeness of a Jew.

[*Enter* **Shylock**]

How now, Shylock! what news among the merchants?

20 **Shylock** You knew, none so well, none so well as you, of my
daughter's flight.

Act three

Scene 1

The street in front of **Shylock**'s *house.* **Solanio** *meets* **Salerio,** *who has just come from the Business Exchange.*

Solario Well, what's the news on the Rialto?

Salerio Why, there's a story going around that one of Antonio's richly laden ships has been wrecked in the Channel – the Goodwins, I think they call the place. A very dangerous and often fatal sandbank, the graveyard of many a fine ship if Madam Rumor is to be trusted.

Solanio I wish she were as big a liar as ever chewed sweets or conned her neighbors into believing she actually mourned the death of her third husband! But it is certainly true, without exaggeration or deviation from the point, that the good Antonio, the honest Antonio – oh that I could describe him adequately! –

Salerio Come on, come to the end of your sentence.

Solanio What's that? What do you say? Well, the end is that he has lost a ship.

Salerio I hope it proves to be the end of his losses.

Solanio Let me say "Amen" at once, in case the devil snarls up my prayer, because here he comes in the shape of a Jew.

[**Shylock** *comes out of his house*]

Well now, Shylock! What news among the merchants?

Shylock [*snapping at him*] You knew – nobody better than you – of my daughter's flight.

Salerio   That's certain! I, for my part, knew the tailor that made the wings she flew withal.

Solanio   And Shylock, for his own part, knew the bird was
25   fledge, and then it is the complexion of them all to leave the dam.

Shylock   She is damned for it.

Salerio   That's certain, if the devil may be her judge.

Shylock   My own flesh and blood to rebel!

30 **Solanio**   Out upon it, old carrion, rebels it at these years?

Shylock   I say my daughter is my flesh and blood.

Salerio   There is more difference between thy flesh and hers than between jet and ivory, more between your bloods than there is between red wine and rhenish. But tell us, do you hear
35   whether Antonio have had any loss at sea or no?

Shylock   There I have another bad match: a bankrupt, a prodigal, who dare scarce show his head on the Rialto; a beggar that was used to come so smug upon the mart. Let him look to his bond! he was wont to call me usurer, let him look to
40   his bond! he was wont to lend money for a Christian curtsy, let him look to his bond!

Salerio   Why, I am sure, if he forfeit, thou wilt not take his flesh: what's that good for?

Shylock   To bait fish withal! if it will feed nothing else, it will
45   feed my revenge. He hath disgraced me and hind'red me half a million, laughed at my losses, mocked at my gains, scorned my nation, thwarted my bargains, cooled my friends, heated mine enemies – and what's his reason? I am a Jew. Hath not a Jew eyes? hath not a Jew hands, organs, dimensions, senses,
50   affections, passions? fed with the same food, hurt with the same weapons, subject to the same diseases, healed by the

Salerio   Oh, for sure! For my part, I knew the tailor who made the wings she flew with!

Solanio   And Shylock, for his part, knew the bird was ready to fly, and that it's only natural for fledglings to leave their mother.

Shylock   She is damned for it!

Salerio   Oh yes – if the devil judges her!

Shylock   My own flesh and blood to rebel!

Solanio   [*deliberately misunderstanding*] Fancy that, you old skin and bones. What, at your age?

Shylock   I mean my daughter, who is my flesh and blood.

Salerio   There's more difference between your flesh and hers than there is between jet black and ivory, more between your bloods than there is between red wine and white. But tell us now [*winking*], have you heard whether Antonio has had any losses at sea or not?

Shylock   There I have another bad deal. A bankrupt. A prodigal. He dares hardly show his face on the Rialto; a beggar now, who used to come so smugly to the market place. He'd better honor his bond! He used to call me a moneylender. He'd better honor his bond! He used to lend money as a Christian favor. He'd better honor his bond!

Salerio   Well, I'm sure if he can't, you will not take his flesh. What good would that be?

Shylock   To bait fish with! If it will feed nothing else, it will feed my revenge. He has disgraced me, and hindered me, half a million times. He has laughed at my losses, mocked at my gains, scorned my nationality, obstructed my deals, alienated my friends, incensed my enemies. And his reason? I am a Jew. Hasn't a Jew got eyes? Hasn't a Jew got hands, organs, limbs, senses, affections, passions? Isn't he fed with the same food,

same means, warmed and cooled by the same winter and
summer, as a Christian is? If you prick us, do we not bleed? if
you tickle us, do we not laugh? if you poison us, do we not
55 die? and if you wrong us, shall we not revenge? if we are like
you in the rest, we will resemble you in that. If a Jew wrong a
Christian, what is his humility? Revenge. If a Christian wrong
a Jew, what should his sufferance be by Christian example?
Why, revenge. The villainy you teach me I will execute, and it
60 shall go hard but I will better the instruction.

[*Enter a* **Servant**]

Servant   Gentlemen, my master Antonio is at his house, and
desires to speak with you both.

Salerio   We have been up and down to seek him.

[*Enter* **Tubal**]

Solanio   Here comes another of the tribe – a third cannot be
65 matched, unless the devil himself turn Jew.

[*Exeunt* **Solanio, Salerio** *and* **Servant**]

Shylock   How now, Tubal! what news from Genoa? Hast thou
found my daughter?

Tubal   I often came where I did hear of her, but cannot find
her.

70 **Shylock**   Why there, there, there, there! A diamond gone, cost
me two thousand ducats in Frankfort! The curse never fell
upon our nation till now, I never felt it till now; two thousand
ducats in that, and other precious, precious jewels. I would
my daughter were dead at my foot, and the jewels in her ear!
75 would she were hearsed at my foot, and the ducats in her
coffin! No news of them? Why, so – and I know not what's

hurt by the same weapons, subject to the same diseases, healed by the same means, warmed and cooled by the same winter and summer, as a Christian is? If you prick us, do we not bleed? If you tickle us, do we not laugh? If you poison us, do we not die? And if you do wrong to us, shall we not seek revenge? If a Jew wrongs a Christian, what is his natural response? Revenge. If a Christian wrongs a Jew, what should his penalty be by Christian example? Why, revenge! The villainy you teach me, I will carry out. And I'll go one better, given half a chance!

[*A* **Servant** *stops* **Solanio** *and* **Salerio**]

Servant   Gentlemen, my master Antonio is at home and would like to speak to you both.

Salerio   We've been looking for him everywhere.

[**Tubal,** *another Jew, is seen making for* **Shylock***'s house*]

Solanio   Here comes another member of the tribe. You couldn't find a suitable third, unless the devil himself turned Jew.

[**Solanio** *and* **Salerio** *leave, followed by the* **Servant**]

Shylock   Greetings, Tubal. What news from Genoa? Have you found my daughter?

Tubal   I often heard her spoken of, but I could not find her.

Shylock   [*suffering aloud*] There, there, there, there! A diamond gone, that cost me two thousand ducats in Frankfurt. The curse upon our nation was never felt till now! I never felt it till now. Two thousand ducats in that and other precious, precious jewels. I wish my daughter were dead at my feet and the ducats in her coffin! No news of them? All right. And I

111

been spent in the search: why, thou loss upon loss! the thief
gone with so much and so much to find the thief, and no
satisfaction, no revenge, nor no ill luck stirring but what
80 lights on my shoulders, no sighs but of my breathing, no tears
but of my shedding.

Tubal   Yes, other men have ill luck too. Antonio, as I heard in
Genoa –

Shylock   What, what, what? ill luck, ill luck?

85 **Tubal**   – hath an argosy cast away, coming from Tripolis.

Shylock   I thank God, I thank God! Is it true? is it true?

Tubal   I spoke with some of the sailors that escaped the wreck.

Shylock   I thank thee good Tubal, good news, good news: ha,
ha! Heard in Genoa?

90 **Tubal**   Your daughter spent in Genoa, as I heard, one night,
fourscore ducats.

Shylock   Thou stick'st a dagger in me. I shall never see my
gold again – fourscore ducats at a sitting! fourscore ducats!

Tubal   There came divers of Antonio's creditors in my
95 company to Venice, that swear he cannot choose but break.

Shylock   I am very glad of it, I'll plague him, I'll torture him, I
am glad of it.

Tubal   One of them showed me a ring that he had of your
daughter for a monkey.

100 **Shylock**   Out upon her! thou torturest me, Tubal – it was my
turquoise – I had it of Leah when I was a bachelor: I would not
have given it for a wilderness of monkeys.

Tubal   But Antonio is certainly undone.

don't know how much the search has cost. Loss upon loss! The thief gone with so much, and so much more spent to find the thief – and no satisfaction! No revenge! No bad luck anywhere except what's burdening my shoulders! No sighs but my sighs! No tears but my tears! [*He cries*]

Tubal   Yes, other men do have bad luck. Antonio, as I heard in Genoa –

Shylock   [*coming to himself again very quickly*] What, what, what? Ill luck? Ill luck?

Tubal   He's lost a merchant ship, coming from Tripoli.

Shylock   I thank God! I thank God! Is it true? Is it true?

Tubal   I spoke to some of the sailors who escaped from the wreck.

Shylock   [*radiant*] I thank you, good Tubal. Good news! Good news! [*He laughs out loud*] Ha! Ha! You heard this in Genoa?

Tubal   [*changing the subject*] In Genoa, your daughter spent (so I'm told) eighty ducats in one night.

Shylock   You stab me with a dagger. I shall never see my gold again. Eighty ducats at a sitting! Eighty ducats!

Tubal   [*swinging back again*] Several of Antonio's creditors were with me in Venice, and they swear he's bound to be bankrupt.

Shylock   I'm glad of it. I'll plague him. I'll torture him. I'm glad of it!

Tubal   [*returning to the subject of* **Jessica**] One of them showed me a ring that your daughter had exchanged with him for a monkey.

Shylock   Damn her! You torture me, Tubal. It was my turquoise ring. Leah gave it me before we were married. I wouldn't have parted with it for a wilderness of monkeys.

Tubal   [*comforting again*] But Antonio is definitely ruined.   113

Shylock Nay, that's true, that's very true, go Tubal, fee me an
105   officer, bespeak him a fortnight before. I will have the heart of
him if he forfeit, for were he out of Venice I can make what
merchandise I will. Go, Tubal, and meet me at our synagogue
– go, good Tubal – at our synagogue, Tubal.

[*Exeunt*]

Scene 2

Portia's house at Belmont. Enter **Bassanio** *with* **Portia, Gratiano**
with **Nerissa,** *and* **Attendants.**

Portia   I pray you tarry: pause a day or two
    Before you hazard, for in choosing wrong
    I lose your company; therefore, forbear awhile.
    There's something tells me, but it is not love,
5   I would not lose you, and you know yourself,
    Hate counsels not in such a quality;
    But lest you should not understand me well –
    And yet a maiden hath no tongue but thought –
    I would detain you here some month or two
10   Before you venture for me. I could teach you
    How to choose right, but then I am forsworn;
    So will I never be, so may you miss me;
    But if you do, you'll make me wish a sin,
    That I had been forsworn. Beshrew your eyes,
15   They have o'er-looked me and divided me,
    One half of me is yours, the other half yours –
    Mine own I would say: but if mine then yours,
    And so all yours. O, these naughty times
    Put bars between the owners and their rights,

Shylock   Yes, that's true. That's very true. Go, Tubal. Engage
me a sheriff. Give him two weeks' notice. I'll have his heart if
he can't pay. Once he's removed from Venice, I can do
business my own way. Go, Tubal, and meet me at our
synagogue. Go, good Tubal – at our synagogue, Tubal . . .

[*They go their ways*]

Scene 2

The hall of **Portia**'*s house in Belmont. The curtains are drawn
back, revealing the caskets. There are musicians seated in the
gallery above.* **Bassanio** *is ready to make his choice.*

Portia   [*obviously in love, but restrained by modesty*] Delay a
little, do. Pause a day or two before you take the gamble. If you
choose wrong, I'll lose your company. Therefore, wait a
while. Something (but it isn't love) tells me I don't want to lose
you – and you know yourself that hatred doesn't give advice
like that! But in case you don't know me well enough (women
can only think their thoughts, not speak out), I'd like to keep
you here a month or two before you make your choice. I could
tell you how to choose the right one, but I'm under oath not to.
If you don't win me, I'll never be another's. If you should fail,
you'll make me wish something sinful – that I had broken my
oath and advised you. Shame on your eyes! They have
bewitched me and divided me in two. One half of me belongs
to you. The other half is yours, too. (I ought to say "my own,"
but what is mine is yours, so all of me is yours.) Oh, these days
owners are often separated from their rights, so though I am

20   And so though yours, not yours. Prove it so,
      Let Fortune go to hell for it, not I.
      I speak too long, but 'tis to peise the time,
      To eke it and to draw it out in length,
      To stay you from election.

Bassanio   Let me choose,
25   For as I am, I live upon the rack.

    Portia   Upon the rack, Bassanio? then confess
    What treason there is mingled with your love.

    Bassanio   None but that ugly treason of mistrust,
    Which makes me fear th'enjoying of my love.
30   There may as well be amity and life
    'Tween snow and fire, as treason and my love.

    Portia   Ay, but I fear you speak upon the rack,
    Where men enforced do speak any thing.

    Bassanio   Promise me life, and I'll confess the truth.

    Portia   Well then, confess and live.

35 **Bassanio**   'Confess' and 'love'
    Had been the very sum of my confession:
    O happy torment, when my torturer
    Doth teach me answers for deliverance!
    But let me to my fortune and the caskets.

40 **Portia**   Away then! I am locked in one of them –
    If you do love me, you will find me out.
    Nerissa and the rest, stand all aloof.
    Let music sound while he doth make his choice –
    Then if he lose, he makes a swan-like end,
45   Fading in music. That the comparison
    May stand more proper, my eye shall be the stream,
    And wat'ry death-bed for him. He may win,
    And what is music then? then music is

yours in one sense, I can't be in reality. Should this be so,
Fortune deserves to go to hell for it, not me! [*She pauses,
embarrassed after this revealing outburst*] I'm going on too
long, but it's to slow time down, to draw it out, and stretch
it longer to delay the making of your choice.

Bassanio   Let me choose. As I am, I'm living on the rack in
torment.

Portia   On the rack, Bassanio! Confess, then, what treason
there is mingled with your love!

Bassanio   None but the ugly treason of mistrust, which makes
me afraid to enjoy my love. Snow and fire might just as well
live in harmony together, as treason and my love.

Portia   Yes, but I'm afraid that being on the rack, you'll say
anything, like any tortured man.

Bassanio   Promise me life, and I'll confess the truth.

Portia   Confess indeed, and live!

Bassanio   "Confess and love" would be my full confession.
What a happy torment, when my torturer tells me the answers
to set me free! But let me test my fortune with the caskets.

Portia   Go then! I am locked in one of them. If you really love
me, you will find me. [*To the onlookers*] Nerissa and the rest of
you, stand to one side. Let music play while he makes his
choice. Then, if he loses, music will accompany him like a
dying swan.

[*One* **Servant** *stays while everyone else goes to the musicians'
gallery*]

To take the comparison further: my tears will be the stream
and watery deathbed for him. [*Taking a more cheerful view*]
He may win. What of music then? Then, music would be like

Even as the flourish when true subjects bow
50 To a new-crowned monarch: such it is,
As are those dulcet sounds in break of day
That creep into the dreaming bridegroom's ear,
And summon him to marriage. Now he goes,
With no less presence, but with much more love,
55 Than young Alcides, when he did redeem
The virgin tribute paid by howling Troy
To the sea-monster. I stand for sacrifice:
The rest aloof are the Dardanian wives,
With bleared visages, come forth to view
60 The issue of th'exploit. Go, Hercules!
Live thou, I live. With much much more dismay
I view the fight than thou that mak'st the fray.

[*A song, whilst* **Bassanio** *comments on the caskets to himself*]

Tell me where is Fancy bred,
Or in the heart, or in the head?
65 How begot, how nourished?

All   Reply, reply.

It is engend'red in the eyes,
With gazing fed, and Fancy dies
In the cradle where it lies.
70   Let us all ring Fancy's knell:
I'll begin it – Ding, dong, bell.

All   Ding, dong, bell.

Bassanio   So may the outward shows be least themselves –
The world is still deceived with ornament.
75 In law, what plea so tainted and corrupt,
But, being seasoned with a gracious voice,
Obscures the show of evil? In religion
What damned error, but some sober brow
Will bless it, and approve it with a text,

the fanfare at a coronation, when loyal subjects bow. Or like
the dawn chorus, that creeps into the dreaming bridegroom's
ear, calling him to his wedding. Then he goes out as
impressive as Hercules (but with much more love in him)
when he rescued Hesione after she'd been offered by the
Trojans to appease the sea-monster. Here, I am the sacrifice.
The observers in the gallery are the Trojan women, tear-
stained, there to see the outcome. [*To* **Bassanio**] Go, Hercules!
If you live, I live. The spectator is suffering more than the
contestant.

[*While* **Bassanio** *considers the caskets, a song is sung*]

Tell me, where is Fancy bred,
In the heart, or in the head?
How begot, how nourished?

Chorus Reply, reply.

It is engendered in the eyes,
With gazing fed. And Fancy dies
In the cradle where it lies.
Let us all ring Fancy's knell:
I'll begin it, Ding, dong, bell.

Chorus Ding, dong, bell.

Bassanio Appearances can be deceptive. The world is always
taken in by ornament. In law, there is no plea, however tainted
or corrupt, whose evil cannot be concealed behind a saintly
voice. In religion, there's no heresy some learned man won't
bless, using the scriptures in support to hide the grossness.

80   Hiding the grossness with fair ornament?
     There is no vice so simple but assumes
     Some mark of virtue on his outward parts.
     How many cowards, whose hearts are all as false
     As stairs of sand, wear yet upon their chins
85   The beards of Hercules and frowning Mars:
     Who, inward searched, have livers white as milk?
     And these assume but valour's excrement
     To render them redoubted. Look on beauty,
     And you shall see 'tis purchased by the weight,
90   Which therein works a miracle in nature,
     Making them lightest that wear most of it:
     So are those crisped snaky golden locks
     Which make such wanton gambols with the wind,
     Upon supposed fairness, often known
95   To be the dowry of a second head,
     The skull that bred them in the sepulchre.
     Thus ornament is but the guiled shore
     To a most dangerous sea; the beauteous scarf
     Veiling an Indian beauty; in a word,
100 The seeming truth which cunning times put on
     To entrap the wisest. Therefore, thou gaudy gold,
     Hard food for Midas, I will none of thee –
     Nor none of thee, thou pale and common drudge
     'Tween man and man: but thou, thou meagre lead,
105 Which rather threaten'st than dost promise aught,
     Thy plainness moves me more than eloquence,
     And here choose I – joy be the consequence!

     Portia   How all the other passions fleet to air,
     As doubtful thoughts, and rash-embraced despair,
110 And shudd'ring fear and green-eyed jealousy!
     O love, be moderate, allay thy ecstasy,
     In measure rein thy joy, scant this excess –
     I feel too much thy blessing, make it less,
     For fear I surfeit!

with fair words. There is no vice, however obvious, that doesn't have some superficial virtue. How many cowards, with hearts as false as stairs made from sand, sport beards like those of Hercules or warlike Mars? Within, their livers are as white as milk. They only grow those beards to make themselves look tough. Consider beauty. You'll see it's often purchased by the ounce. Cosmetics work miracles: those with the lightest morals use them most heavily! Similarly, those golden wavy tresses that look so fetching in the wind, so glamorous, are often made from hair taken from the head of one now dead and buried. Ornament is the treacherous shore of a very dangerous sea, the beautiful scarf veiling an uncertain beauty; in short, it is a mock-truth that on swindling occasions can deceive the cleverest of men. Therefore, gaudy gold, food for Midas, I want none of you. Nor of you, silver, the stuff of common currency. But you, worthless lead, which threatens rather than promises, your plain speaking appeals more than the eloquence of your rivals. This is my choice. [*The* **Servant** *hands him the key*] May it bring happiness!

Portia   [*aside*] How quickly every other passion vanishes: doubt, unjustified despair, shuddering fear and green-eyed jealousy! Oh, love, be moderate, control your ecstasy; restrain your joy. Don't get too excited – your blessing overwhelms me. Make it less, in case it swamps me!

Bassanio   What find I here?
115   Fair Portia's counterfeit! What demi-god
      Hath come so near creation? Move these eyes?
      Or whether, riding on the balls of mine,
      Seem they in motion? Here are severed lips,
      Parted with sugar breath: so sweet a bar
120   Should sunder such sweet friends. Here in her hairs
      The painter plays the spider, and hath woven
      A golden mesh t'entrap the hearts of men,
      Faster than gnats in cobwebs; but her eyes!
      How could he see to do them? having made one,
125   Methinks it should have power to steal both his,
      And leave itself unfurnished: yet look, how far
      The substance of my praise doth wrong this shadow
      In underprizing it, so far this shadow
      Doth limp behind the substance. Here's the scroll,
130   The continent and summary of my fortune.

          'You that choose not by the view,
          Chance as fair and choose as true:
          Since this fortune falls to you,
          Be content, and seek no new.
135   If you be well pleased with this,
          And hold your fortune for your bliss,
          Turn you where your lady is,
          And claim her with a loving kiss.'

      A gentle scroll! Fair lady, by your leave;
140   I come by note, to give and to receive.
      Like one of two contending in a prize,
      That thinks he hath done well in people's eyes,
      Hearing applause and universal shout,
      Giddy in spirit, still gazing in a doubt
145   Whether those peals of praise be his or no,
      So, thrice-fair lady stand I, even so,
      As doubtful whether what I see be true,
      Until confirmed, signed, ratified by you.

Bassanio   [*opening the casket*] What do I find here? Fair
Portia's portrait! [*Admiring it*] How close to the divine this is!
Do these eyes move? Or are they only reflecting the motion of
my own? Here are lips parted with sugar breath: sweetness
separates sweet things! Here in her hair the painter has, like a
spider, woven a golden net to entrap men's hearts, faster than
gnats in cobwebs. But her eyes! How could he see to do them?
After he painted one, that eye might have blinded both of his
and denied itself a companion. But look! Just as my praises
undervalue the portrait, the portrait falls short of the reality.
Here's the scroll, on which my fortune's summarized:

> You who choose not by the view
> Take fair chance, and choose quite true:
> Since this fortune falls to you
> Be content, seek nothing new.
> If you be well pleased with this,
> And see your fortune as your bliss,
> Turn to where your lady is,
> And claim her with a loving kiss.

A kindly scroll! [*He turns to* **Portia**] Fair lady, with your
permission I come to you with a permit [*offering the scroll as
his passport to a kiss*] to give and to receive. [*But he is too shy
to proceed*] I'm like a man competing with another for a prize.
He thinks he's pleased the public, hearing applause and
cheering. But somewhat dizzy, he looks doubtful, wondering
whether the clapping is for him or not. That's how I stand,
thrice beautiful lady: doubtful whether my eyes are deceiving
me; waiting for your confirmation, your signature, your
consent.

Portia   You see me, Lord Bassanio, where I stand,
150   Such as I am: though for myself alone
I would not be ambitious in my wish
To wish myself much better: yet for you
I would be trebled twenty times myself:
A thousand times more fair, ten thousand times
155   More rich;
That only to stand high in your account,
I might in virtues, beauties, livings, friends,
Exceed account. But the full sum of me
In some of something which, to term in gross,
160   Is an unlessoned girl, unschooled, unpractised;
Happy in this, she is not yet so old
But she may learn; happier than this,
She is not bred so dull but she can learn;
Happiest of all is that her gentle spirit
165   Commits itself to yours to be directed,
As from her lord, her governor, her king.
Myself and what is mine to you and yours
Is now converted. But now I was the lord
Of this fair mansion, master of my servants,
170   Queen o'er myself; and even now, but now,
This house, these servants, and this same myself,
Are yours – my lord's – I give them with this ring,
Which when you part from, lose, or give away,
Let it presage the ruin of your love,
175   And be my vantage to exclaim on you.

Bassanio   Madam, you have bereft me of all words,
Only my blood speaks to you in my veins,
And there is such confusion in my powers
As, after some oration fairly spoke
180   By a beloved prince, there doth appear
Among the buzzing pleased multitude,
Where every something, being blent together,
Turns to a wild of nothing, save of joy,

Portia   You see me, Lord Bassanio, where I stand – such as I am. For myself, I do not seek improvement. But for you, I wish I were sixty times better than I am, a thousand times more beautiful, ten thousand times richer. To earn your highest regard, would that I could increase my present worth of virtue, beauty, wealth and friends. In my entirety, I'm really very little – at best an uneducated girl, untrained, inexperienced. Happily, not too old to learn. Happier still, not too stupid to learn. Happiest of all – she surrenders herself to your instruction. You are her lord, her governor, her king. [**Bassanio** and **Portia** *kiss, fulfilling the terms of the scroll*] Myself and all I own is now transferred to you and yours. Until just now, I was the lord of this fine house; the master of my servants, queen of my own destiny. Suddenly, this house, these servants and I myself are yours – my lord's! I give them with this ring. [*She places one on* **Bassanio's** *finger*] Should you part with it, or give it away, it will signify the end of your love and be my reason for denouncing you.

Bassanio   Madam, I don't know what to say. The blood in my veins alone can speak to you. I'm as overcome as when a rapturous crowd is addressed by a beloved monarch. It shouts out in unison. Each individual enthusiastic cry blends with the rest to form a wild tumult of joy expressed without words.

185 Expressed and not expressed. But when this ring
     Parts from this finger, then parts life from hence!
     O, then be bold to say Bassanio's dead.

Nerissa   My lord and lady, it is now our time,
     That have stood by and seen our wishes prosper,
     To cry good joy. Good joy, my lord and lady!

190 **Gratiano**   My Lord Bassanio, and my gentle lady,
     I wish you all the joy that you can wish;
     For I am sure you can wish none from me:
     And, when your honours mean to solemnize
     The bargain of your faith, I do beseech you,
195 Even at that time I may be married too.

Bassanio   With all my heart, so thou canst get a wife.

Gratiano   I thank your lordship, you have got me one.
     My eyes, my lord, can look as swift as yours:
     You saw the mistress, I beheld the maid;
200 You loved, I loved – for intermission
     No more pertains to me, my lord, than you;
     Your fortune stood upon the caskets there,
     And so did mine too, as the matter falls:
     For wooing here until I sweat again,
205 And swearing till my very roof was dry
     With oaths of love, at last – if promise last –
     I got a promise of this fair one here,
     To have her love, provided that your fortune
     Achieved her mistress.

Portia   Is this true, Nerissa?

210 **Nerissa**   Madam, it is, so you stand pleased withal.

Bassanio   And do you, Gratiano, mean good faith?

Gratiano   Yes, faith, my lord.

When this ring parts from this finger, life itself will end. Then you could confidently say: "This means Bassanio is dead."

[**Nerissa** *and* **Gratiano** *join them*]

Nerissa   My lord and lady: now is the time for those who've watched, and seen their wishes come true, to cry "Good joy!" Good joy, my lord and lady!

Gratiano   Lord Bassanio, and my gentle lady, I wish you all the joy you wish yourselves, for I am sure you don't need mine. And when the time comes for your wedding, at the same time, with your permission, may I be married too!

Bassanio   Wholeheartedly – if you can find a wife.

Gratiano   Thanking your lordship – you have found me one. [*He takes* **Nerissa***'s hand*] My eyes, my lord, are just as swift as yours. You saw the mistress: I spotted the maid. You loved, I loved. I needed no more prompting than you, my lord. Your fortune depended on the caskets there, and so did mine, as it happened. After wooing till I sweated, and swearing oaths of love till my mouth ran dry, at last – if promises last! – I got a promise of her hand from this fair lady here on condition you won the mistress.

Portia   [*delighted*] Is this true, Nerissa?

Nerissa   Madam, it is, if you approve.

Bassanio   Are you in earnest, Gratiano?

Gratiano   Yes indeed, my lord.

Bassanio   Our feast shall be much honoured in your marriage.

Gratiano   We'll play with them the first boy for a thousand
215   ducats.

Nerissa   What, and stake down?

Gratiano   No, we shall ne'er win at that sport, and stake down.

[*Enter* **Lorenzo, Jessica,** *and* **Salerio**]

But who comes here? Lorenzo and his infidel?
What, and my old Venetian friend, Salerio?

220   **Bassanio**   Lorenzo and Salerio, welcome hither,
If that the youth of my new interest here
Have power to bid you welcome. By your leave,
I bid my very friends and countrymen,
Sweet Portia, welcome.

Portia   So do I, my lord.
225   They are entirely welcome.

Lorenzo   I thank your honour. For my part, my lord,
My purpose was not to have seen you here,
But meeting with Salerio by the way,
He did entreat me, past all saying nay,
To come with him along.

230   **Salerio**   I did, my lord,
And I have reason for it. Signior Antonio
Commends him to you.

[*He gives* **Bassanio** *a letter*]

Bassanio   Ere I ope his letter,
I pray you, tell me how my good friend doth.

Bassanio Our wedding feast will be most honored by you marriage.

Gratiano [*to* **Nerissa**] We'll wager them a thousand ducats have a son first.

Nerissa [*blushing*] What, betting on that?

Gratiano [*deliberately mishearing*] We'll never win at that game, if we don't do some petting!

[**Lorenzo** *and* **Jessica**, *followed by* **Salerio**, *join them*]

But who comes here? Lorenzo and his Jewess? What, and my old Venetian friend, Salerio?

Bassanio Lorenzo and Salerio, welcome, if one so new in status here can so presume. [*To* **Portia**] With your permission, sweet Portia, I welcome my good friends and countrymen.

Portia So do I, my lord. They are extremely welcome.

Lorenzo [*to* **Bassanio**] I thank your honor. For my part, my lord, I didn't plan to see you here. But I met Salerio on the way, and he begged me to come along with him. He wouldn't take no for an answer.

Salerio I did, my lord, and with good reason. [*He gives* **Bassanio** *a letter*] Signior Antonio sends his respects.

Bassanio Before I open this letter, tell me how my good friend is?

Salerio   Not sick, my lord, unless it be in mind –
Nor well, unless in mind: his letter there
235   Will show you his estate.

Gratiano   Nerissa, cheer yon stranger, bid her welcome.
Your hand, Salerio. What's the news from Venice?
How doth that royal merchant, good Antonio?
I know he will be glad of our success,
240   We are the Jasons, we have won the fleece.

Salerio   I would you had won the fleece that he hath lost.

Portia   There are some shrewd contents in yon same paper,
That steals the colour from Bassanio's cheek:
Some dear friend dead, else nothing in the world
245   Could turn so much the constitution
Of any constant man. What, worse and worse!
With leave, Bassanio – I am half yourself,
And I must freely have the half of anything
That this same paper brings you.

Bassanio   O sweet Portia,
250   Here are a few of the unpleasant'st words
That ever blotted paper. Gentle lady,
When I did first impart my love to you,
I freely told you all the wealth I had
Ran in my veins. I was a gentleman –
255   And then I told you true: and yet, dear lady,
Rating myself at nothing, you shall see
How much I was a braggart. When I told you
My state was nothing, I should then have told you
That I was worse than nothing; for, indeed,
260   I have engaged myself to a dear friend,
Engaged my friend to his mere enemy,
To feed my means. Here is a letter, lady,
The paper as the body of my friend,
And every word in it a gaping wound,

Salerio Not sick, my lord, unless it's in his mind. He's not well, either, unless you mean mentally. His letter explains his situation.

[**Bassanio** *opens the letter*]

Gratiano [*nodding in the direction of* **Jessica**] Nerissa, cheer up our stranger. Make her welcome! [**Nerissa** *greets* **Jessica**, *while* **Gratiano** *shakes hands with* **Salerio**] Your hand, Salerio. What news from Venice? How is that royal merchant, good Antonio? I know he will be glad of our success. We are the Jasons! We have won the fleece!

Salerio Would that you had won the fleece that he has lost. [*He takes* **Gratiano** *to one side to explain*]

Portia [*observing* **Bassanio** *as he reads*] There must be something very important in that letter to turn him so pale. A dear friend must have died. Nothing else in the world could upset a stable man so much. [**Bassanio** *looks even more distressed as she speaks*] What, worse and worse? [*She lays her hand on his arm*] With respect, Bassanio. I am half yourself. I will readily share the half of anything this letter brings you.

Bassanio Oh, sweet Portia! [*He is overcome with grief*] Here are some of the most unpleasant words that ever blotted paper. Gentle lady, when I first revealed my love for you, I freely told you all the wealth I owned was in my veins. I was a gentleman, and I told you the truth. And yet, dear lady, in rating myself at zero, you will see how boastful I was. When I told you I had nothing, I should have added I was worse than nothing. Actually, I'm indebted to a dear friend, ar 1 to swell my funds I've made my friend indebted to his worst enemy. [*He chokes his tears*] Here is a letter, lady. The paper represents the body of my friend, and every word written on it is a gaping wound, leaking lifeblood. [*To* **Salerio**] Is this true,

265   Issuing life-blood. But is it true, Salerio?
    Have all his ventures failed? What, not one hit?
    From Tripolis, from Mexico, and England,
    From Lisbon, Barbary, and India?
    And not one vessel scape the dreadful touch
    Of merchant-marring rocks?

270 **Salerio**   Not one, my lord.
    Besides, it should appear, that if he had
    The present money to discharge the Jew,
    He would not take it. Never did I know
    A creature that did bear the shape of man
275   So keen and greedy to confound a man:
    He plies the duke at morning and at night,
    And doth impeach the freedom of the state,
    If they deny him justice. Twenty merchants,
    The duke himself, and the magnificoes
280   Of greatest port, have all persuaded with him,
    But none can drive him from the envious plea
    Of forfeiture, of justice, and his bond.

    Jessica   When I was with him, I have heard him swear
    To Tubal and to Chus, his countrymen,
285   That he would rather have Antonio's flesh
    Than twenty times the value of the sum
    That he did owe him: and I know, my lord,
    If law, authority, and power, deny not,
    It will go hard with poor Antonio.

290 **Portia**   Is it your dear friend that is thus in trouble?

    Bassanio   The dearest friend to me, the kindest man,
    The best-conditioned and unwearied spirit
    In doing courtesies; and one in whom
    The ancient Roman honour more appears
295   Than any that draws breath in Italy.

Salerio? Have all his investments failed? Not one success?
From Tripoli, Mexico and England, from Lisbon, Barbary and
India? And not one vessel has survived the fearful touch of
shipwrecking rocks?

Salerio   Not one, my lord. And there is more to it: it seems that
even if he had the money to discharge his debt to the Jew, he
would not take it. I never knew a creature in human form so
sharp and hungry to destroy a man. He appeals to the duke
from morning till night. He says it is against the constitution to
deny him justice. Twenty merchants, the duke, and the richest
of the nobility have all argued with him. But none can shift him
from his vengeful plea of forfeiture, of justice and his bond.

Jessica   When I lived with him, I heard him swear to Tubal and
to Chus, his countrymen, that he would rather have Antonio's
flesh than twenty times the money that he owed him. I know,
my lord, that if law, authority and power don't stop him,
Antonio is in grave danger.

Portia   Is it your dear friend who is in this trouble?

Bassanio   My dearest friend. The kindest man, the best
meaning and most tireless of those who do good turns. One
with more Roman honor about him than any man in Italy.

Portia   What sum owes he the Jew?

Bassanio   For me, three thousand ducats.

Portia   What, no more?
Pay him six thousand, and deface the bond;
Double six thousand, and then treble that,
300   Before a friend of this description
Shall lose a hair through Bassanio's fault.
First go with me to church and call me wife,
And then away to Venice to your friend;
For never shall you lie by Portia's side
305   With an unquiet soul. You shall have gold
To pay the petty debt twenty times over.
When it is paid, bring your true friend along.
My maid Nerissa and myself meantime
Will live as maids and widows. Come, away!
310   For you shall hence upon your wedding-day:
Bid your friends welcome, show a merry cheer:
Since you are dear bought, I will love you dear.
But let me hear the letter of your friend.

Bassanio   'Sweet Bassanio, my ships have all miscarried, my
315   creditors grow cruel, my estate is very low, my bond to the
Jew is forfeit, and since, in paying it, it is impossible I should
live, all debts are cleared between you and I, if I might but see
you at my death: notwithstanding, use your pleasure – if your
love do not persuade you to come, let not my letter.'

320 **Portia**   O love, dispatch all business and be gone!

Bassanio   Since I have your good leave to go away,
I will make haste; but, till I come again,
No bed shall e'er be guilty of my stay,
Nor rest be interposer 'twixt us twain.

[*Exeunt*]

Portia   How much does he owe the Jew?

Bassanio   On my behalf, three thousand ducats.

Portia   No more? Pay him six thousand, and reclaim the bond. Twice six thousand. Three times that. No friend of that description shall lose a hair of his head through the fault of Bassanio. [*Decisively*] First, go with me to church and marry me. Then, leave for Venice and your friend. You shall not sleep with Portia with an uneasy mind. You'll have enough gold to pay the petty debt twenty times over. When it is paid, bring your true friend back with you. Meanwhile, my maid Nerissa and I will live like maids and widows. Away, now! You must depart on your wedding day. Bid welcome to your friends! Look cheerful! Since you are dearly bought, I'll love you dearly. Let me hear your friend's letter.

Bassanio   [*reading*] "Dear Bassanio. My ships have all miscarried. My creditors grow cruel. My assets are very low. My bond to the Jew is forfeit. In repaying it, I cannot possibly live. But all debts between us will be cleared if, at my death, I could but see you. Nonetheless, do as you wish. If your love for me does not persuade you to come, don't let this letter change your mind."

Portia   Oh, my love! Settle your affairs and begone!

Bassanio   Since I have your consent to go, I'll make all haste. Till I return, I'll let neither bed nor sleep come between us.

[*They hurry off*]

Scene 3

Outside Shylock's house. Enter **Shylock, Solanio, Antonio,** *and a* **Gaoler.**

Shylock   Gaoler, look to him: tell not me of mercy;
This is the fool that lent out money gratis.
Gaoler, look to him.

Antonio   Hear me yet, good Shylock.

Shylock   I'll have my bond; speak not against my bond.
5   I have sworn an oath that I will have my bond:
Thou call'dst me dog before thou hadst a cause,
But since I am a dog, beware my fangs.
The duke shall grant me justice. I do wonder,
Thou naughty gaoler, that thou art so fond
10   To come abroad with him at his request.

Antonio   I pray thee, hear me speak.

Shylock   I'll have my bond; I will not hear thee speak.
I'll have my bond, and therefore speak no more.
I'll not be made a soft and dull-eyed fool,
15   To shake the head, relent, and sigh, and yield
To Christian intercessors. Follow not;
I'll have no speaking, I will have my bond.

[*Exit*]

Solanio   It is the most impenetrable cur,
That ever kept with men.

Antonio   Let him alone,
20   I'll follow him no more with bootless prayers.
He seeks my life – his reason well I know;
I oft delivered from his forfeitures

Scene 3

The street outside **Shylock's** *house.* **Shylock** *stands at the door, with* **Antonio, Solanio** *and a* **Jailer.**

Shylock   Jailer – guard him well! [*Gesturing wildly*] Don't speak to me about mercy! This is the fool who lent out money free of interest. Jailer, guard him.

Antonio   Listen a moment, good Shylock –

Shylock   I'll have my bond! Don't speak against my bond! I've sworn an oath that I will have my bond! You called me "dog" before you had a reason. Since I am a dog, beware my teeth! The duke will grant me justice. I'm amazed, you wicked jailer, that you are so foolish as to wander about with him at his request!

Antonio   Please hear me speak!

Shylock   [*shouting*] I'll have my bond! I won't hear you speak! I'll have my bond, so say no more. I'll not be made a soft and stupid fool: shaking my head, relenting, sighing – and yielding to Christian entreaties! [*He turns to go inside*] Don't follow me! Don't talk to me! I'll have my bond! [*He enters his house, slamming the door*]

Solanio   He's the most obstinate dog that ever lived in human company!

Antonio   Leave him alone. I'll follow him no more with useless pleas. He wants my life. I know his reason well. I often

Many that have at times made moan to me;
Therefore he hates me.

Solanio   I am sure the duke
25 Will never grant this forfeiture to hold.

Antonio   The duke cannot deny the course of law:
For the commodity that strangers have
With us in Venice, if it be denied,
Will much impeach the justice of the state,
30 Since that the trade and profit of the city
Consisteth of all nations. Therefore, go:
These griefs and losses have so bated me
That I shall hardly spare a pound of flesh
Tomorrow to my bloody creditor.
35 Well, gaoler, on. Pray God, Bassanio come
To see me pay his debt, and then I care not!

[*Exeunt*]

Scene 4

Portia's house at Belmont. Enter **Portia, Nerissa, Lorenzo,
Jessica,** *and* **Balthazar.**

Lorenzo   Madam, although I speak it in your presence,
You have a noble and a true conceit
Of god-like amity, which appears most strongly
In bearing thus the absence of your lord.
5 But if you knew to whom you show this honour,
How true a gentleman you send relief,
How dear a lover of my lord your husband,
I know you would be prouder of the work
Than customary bounty can enforce you.

discharged the debts of people who asked me for help. So he hates me.

Solanio   I'm sure the duke will never rule in favor of this forfeiture.

Antonio   The duke can't change the course of law. If we denied the rights of foreigners here in Venice, it would go against our notions of impartial justice. The city has commercial links with people of all nations. So, go. I've lost so much weight through worry and my losses, that I'll scarcely have a pound of flesh to spare tomorrow for my bloodthirsty creditor. Well, Jailer, let's move on. Please God, Bassanio will come to see me pay his debt. Then I shall be content!

[*They go*]

Scene 4

Portia*'s house in Belmont. Enter* **Portia, Nerissa, Lorenzo, Jessica,** *and* **Portia***'s servant* **Balthazar***. They have been discussing love and friendship.*

Lorenzo   [*very sincerely*] Madam, although I say it in your presence, you have a truly noble understanding of friendship. It's obvious from the way you can accept your husband's absence. But if you knew the man you are honoring; how true a gentleman he is, how dearly he loves my lord your husband, I know you would be even prouder than ordinary goodwill would demand.

10 **Portia**   I never did repent for doing good,
    Nor shall not now: for in companions
    That do converse and waste the time together,
    Whose souls do bear an equal yoke of love,
    There must be needs a like proportion
15   Of lineaments, of manners, and of spirit;
    Which makes me think that this Antonio,
    Being the bosom lover of my lord,
    Must needs be like my lord. If it be so,
    How little is the cost I have bestowed
20   In purchasing the semblance of my soul
    From out the state of hellish cruelty?
    This comes too near the praising of myself,
    Therefore no more of it: hear other things.
    Lorenzo, I commit into your hands
25   The husbandry and manage of my house,
    Until my lord's return: for mine own part,
    I have toward heaven breathed a secret vow
    To live in prayer and contemplation,
    Only attended by Nerissa here,
30   Until her husband and my lord's return.
    There is a monastery two miles off,
    And there we will abide. I do desire you
    Not to deny this imposition,
    The which my love and some necessity
35   Now lays upon you.

Lorenzo   Madam, with all my heart
    I shall obey you in all fair commands.

Portia   My people do already know my mind,
    And will acknowledge you and Jessica
    In place of Lord Bassanio and myself.
40   So fare you well till we shall meet again.

Lorenzo   Fair thoughts and happy hours attend on you!

Portia I've never regretted doing good and do not now.
Between friends who chat and spend their time together, and
who love each other equally, there must be a similarity in
character, style and spirit. This makes me think that Antonio,
being the bosom friend of my husband, must therefore be like
him. If that's the case, how cheaply have I rescued a soul mate
from hellish cruelty. But this is getting too close to self-praise,
so that's enough of that! To change the subject. Lorenzo, I
want you to take full charge of my household until my
husband returns. For myself, I've made a secret vow to God to
live in prayer and contemplation alone, except for Nerissa
here, until our husbands return. There is a monastery two
miles away. We'll live there. I hope you won't deny me my
request: an imposition based on love and pressing need.

Lorenzo [*bowing*] Madam, I shall always do my best to oblige
you.

Portia My servants already know my plans and will accept you
and Jessica in place of me and Lord Bassanio. So goodbye till
we meet again!

Lorenzo Sweet thoughts and happy hours be yours!

Jessica   I wish your ladyship all heart's content.

Portia   I thank you for your wish, and am well pleased
To wish it back on you: fare you well, Jessica.

[*Exeunt* **Jessica** *and* **Lorenzo**]

45   Now, Balthazar,
As I have ever found thee honest-true,
So let me find thee still. Take this same letter,
And use thou all th'endeavour of a man
In speed to Padua; see thou render this
50   Into my cousin's hand, Doctor Bellario,
And look what notes and garments he doth give thee,
Bring them, I pray thee, with imagined speed
Unto the tranect, to the common ferry
Which trades to Venice. Waste no time in words,
55   But get thee gone. I shall be there before thee.

Balthazar   Madam, I go with all convenient speed.

[*Exit*]

Portia   Come on, Nerissa: I have work in hand
That you yet know not of; we'll see our husbands
Before they think of us.

Nerissa   Shall they see us?

60   **Portia**   They shall, Nerissa; but in such a habit
That they shall think we are accomplished
With that we lack. I'll hold thee any wager,
When we are both accoutred like young men,
I'll prove the prettier fellow of the two,
65   And wear my dagger with the braver grace,
And speak between the change of man and boy
With a reed voice, and turn two mincing steps

Jessica   I wish all heart's contentment to your ladyship!

Portia   Thank you: I'm more than happy to wish the same to you. Goodbye, Jessica! [**Jessica** *and* **Lorenzo** *leave*] Now, Balthazar! I've always found you honest and faithful. May you be so now. [*Handing over a letter*] Take this letter, and get to Padua as quickly as you can. Deliver it to my cousin, Doctor Bellario, and he'll give you certain documents and clothing. Bring them, I pray you, with lightning speed to the crossing where the public ferry trades with Venice. Don't stop to speak, just go. I'll be there before you.

Balthazar   Madam, I'll make haste.

[*He departs*]

Portia   Come on, Nerissa. I have work to do that is as yet unknown to you. We'll see our husbands before they think of us.

Nerissa   Will they see us?

Portia   They will, Nerissa, but they'll think by our dress that we are male. I'll bet you that when we're dressed like young men, I'll be the handsomer of the two. I'll wear my dagger more jauntily, speak with a high-pitched voice like an adolescent –

Into a manly stride; and speak of frays
Like a fine bragging youth; and tell quaint lies,
70   How honourable ladies sought my love,
Which I denying, they fell sick and died;
I could not do withal; then I'll repent,
And wish, for all that, that I had not killed them.
And twenty of these puny lies I'll tell,
75   That men shall swear I have discontinued school
Above a twelvemonth. I have within my mind
A thousand raw tricks of these bragging Jacks,
Which I will practise.

Nerissa   Why, shall we turn to men?

Portia   Fie, what a question's that,
80   If thou wert near a lewd interpreter!
But come, I'll tell thee all my whole device,
When I am in my coach, which stays for us
At the park gate; and therefore haste away,
For we must measure twenty miles today.

                                                    [*Exeunt*]

Scene 5

The garden of Portia's house. Enter **Lancelot** *and* **Jessica**.

Lancelot   Yes truly, for look you, the sins of the father are to
be laid upon the children: therefore, I promise you, I fear
you. I was always plain with you, and so now I speak my
agitation of the matter: therefore, be o' good cheer, for truly I
5   think you are damned. There is but one hope in it that can do
you any good, and that is but a kind of bastard hope neither.

turn my maidenly steps into a manly stride, speak of brawls like a youthful braggart, tell white lies about how chaste ladies pursued me but fell sick and died when I turned them down (lacking the necessary equipment)! Then I'll repent and wish I hadn't killed them. I'll tell twenty such petty lies, so that people will accept I left school at least twelve months ago! In my head I have a thousand tall stories to tell, like a boastful young fellow.

Nerissa   What, are we to turn into men?

Portia   Dear me! What kind of question would that be if there were a lewd-minded person around! But come, I'll tell you my entire plan when I'm in my coach, which is waiting for us at the park gate. So let's hurry away. We must cover twenty miles today.

[*They rush away*]

Scene 5

The garden of **Portia**'s *house at Belmont.* **Lancelot** *is cheerfully explaining to* **Jessica** *his theories about non-Christians.*

Lancelot   Yes, really, because the sins of the father are visited upon the children, I fear for you. I've always spoken frankly to you. Now I tell you my considered opinion. Be of good cheer. Honestly, I think you are damned. There's only one glimmer of hope in this to do you any good, and that's rather an illegitimate hope.

Jessica   And what hope is that, I pray thee?

Lancelot   Marry, you may partly hope that your father got you not, that you are not the Jew's daughter.

10 **Jessica**   That were a kind of bastard hope, indeed! So the sins of my mother should be visited upon me.

Lancelot   Truly then I fear you are damned both by father and mother: thus when I shun Scylla, your father, I fall into Charybdis, your mother: well, you are gone both ways.

15 **Jessica**   I shall be saved by my husband – he hath made me a Christian.

Lancelot   Truly, the more to blame he. We were Christians enow before, e'en as many as could well live, one by another. This making of Christians will raise the price of hogs: if we
20   grow all to be pork-eaters, we shall not shortly have a rasher on the coals for money.

[*Enter* **Lorenzo**]

Jessica   I'll tell my husband, Lancelot, what you say: here he comes.

Lorenzo   I shall grow jealous of you shortly, Lancelot, if you
25   thus get my wife into corners.

Jessica   Nay, you need not fear us, Lorenzo. Lancelot and I are out. He tells me flatly there's no mercy for me in heaven, because I am a Jew's daughter: and he says you are no good member of the commonwealth, for, in converting Jews to
30   Christians, you raise the price of pork.

Lorenzo   I shall answer that better to the commonwealth than you can the getting up of the negro's belly: the Moor is with child by you, Lancelot.

Jessica   And what hope is that, pray?

Lancelot   Well, you could partly hope that your father isn't your father, and that you aren't the Jew's daughter.

Jessica   That's a bastard sort of hope, indeed! So the sins of my mother would be visited upon me!

Lancelot   [*thinks*] Frankly, then I fear you are damned by your father and your mother. So, when I turn away from Scylla, your father, I encounter Charybdis, your mother. You have had it both ways.

Jessica   I shall be saved by my husband. He has made me a Christian.

Lancelot   Truly, the more blame to him. We had enough Christians before. Quite as many as could live comfortably side by side. This making of Christians will raise the price of pigs. If we all start eating pork, in no time we'll not be able to afford to cook bacon!

[**Lorenzo** *comes from the house*]

Jessica   I'll tell my husband, Lancelot, what you say. Here he comes!

Lorenzo   I'll be getting jealous of you soon, Lancelot, if you persist in getting my wife into a corner.

Jessica   No, you needn't fear us, Lorenzo. Lancelot and I aren't friends. He tells me flatly that there's no mercy for me in heaven, because I'm a Jew's daughter. And he says you aren't a good member of the nation because, in converting Jews to Christians, you are raising the price of pork!

Lorenzo   Easier to explain that to the nation than account for the pregnancy of that Negro woman in the news today. You must be to blame for that.

147

Lancelot   It is much that the Moor should be more than
35   reason: but if she be less than an honest woman, she is indeed
more than I took her for.

Lorenzo   How every fool can play upon the word! I think the
best grace of wit will shortly turn into silence, and discourse
grow commendable in none only but parrots. Go in, sirrah:
40   bid them prepare for dinner.

Lancelot   That is done, sir: they have all stomachs.

Lorenzo   Goodly Lord, what a wit-snapper are you! then bid
them prepare dinner.

Lancelot   That is done too, sir – only 'cover' is the word.

45 **Lorenzo**   Will you cover then, sir?

Lancelot   Not so, sir, neither – I know my duty.

Lorenzo   Yet more quarrelling with occasion! Wilt thou show
the whole wealth of thy wit in an instant. I pray thee,
understand a plain man in his plain meaning: go to thy
50   fellows, bid them cover the table, serve in the meat, and we
will come in to dinner.

Lancelot   For the table, sir, it shall be served in – for the meat,
sir, it shall be covered; for your coming in to dinner, sir, why,
let it be as humours and conceits shall govern.

[*Exit*]

55 **Lorenzo**   O dear discretion, how his words are suited!
The fool hath planted in his memory
An army of good words, and I do know
A many fools that stand in better place
Garnished like him, that for a tricksy word
60   Defy the matter. How cheer'st thou, Jessica?
And now, good sweet, say thy opinion,
How dost thou like the Lord Bassanio's wife?

Lancelot It's very strange that a virgin should be expecting. But if she's no better than she should be, she is indeed worse than I took her for

Lorenzo How all comedians play upon words! Some day, true wit will be silenced. Conversation will only be allowed among parrots. Go in, fool! Tell the servants to prepare for dinner!

Lancelot That's done, sir: they are all hungry.

Lorenzo Good lord, what a clown you are! All right – ask them to *prepare* dinner.

Lancelot That's done, too, sir – we only need to put the cloth on.

Lorenzo [*pointing to* **Lancelot***'s hat*] Will you put that on, then?

Lancelot Oh no, sir, no [*pretending to be humble*] – I know my manners.

Lorenzo Yet more quibbling! Are you trying to dazzle us with your quick wit? Please understand a plain man's meaning. [*Patiently*] Go to your fellow-servants, tell them to lay the cloth on the table and serve the meat. Then we will come in to dinner.

Lancelot [*counting each item on his fingers*] As for the table, we'll serve it; as for the meat, it shall be laid on the cloth; as for your coming in to dinner, well, sir, let that be as the fancy takes you.

[*He goes inside*]

Lorenzo How aptly he plays with words! The fool has a good verbal memory. I know many famous comedians who make slick retorts but no sense. Cheer up, Jessica! And now, sweetheart, tell me this: How do you like Bassanio's wife?

Jessica   Past all expressing. It is very meet,
The Lord Bassanio live an upright life,
65   For having such a blessing in his lady
He finds the joys of heaven here on earth,
And if on earth he do not merit it,
In reason he should never come to heaven!
Why, if two gods should play some heavenly match,
70   And on the wager lay two earthly women,
And Portia one, there must be something else
Pawned with the other, for the poor rude world
Hath not her fellow.

Lorenzo   Even such a husband
Hast thou of me, as she is for a wife.

75 **Jessica**   Nay, but ask my opinion too of that.

Lorenzo   I will anon – first, let us go to dinner.

Jessica   Nay, let me praise you while I have a stomach.

Lorenzo   No, pray thee, let it serve for table-talk;
Then, howsome'er thou speak'st, 'mong other things
I shall digest it.

80 **Jessica**   Well, I'll set you forth.

[*Exeunt*]

Jessica Beyond all words! Lord Bassanio must live virtuously, for with this lady he enjoys a heaven here on earth. And if on earth he doesn't value her, he'll never go to heaven! Indeed, if two gods were to play some heavenly game with two earthly women as their bets, and Portia were one of them, there would have to be some extra offered with the other. This poor, simple world could not supply her equal.

Lorenzo [*teasing*] Just such a husband am I to you as she is as a wife. . . .

Jessica You must ask me about that!

Lorenzo I will soon. First, let's go to dinner.

Jessica No, let me praise you while I have the appetite for it!

Lorenzo No, you may as well keep it for table talk. Then, no matter what you say, I can digest it.

Jessica Well, I'll set it all out for you!

[*They go in to dinner, laughing*]

Act four

Scene 1

A Court of Justice in Venice. Enter **Antonio, Bassanio, Gratiano, Solanio,** *and others. The* **Duke** *follows them.*

Duke   What, is Antonio here?

Antonio   Ready, so please your grace.

Duke   I am sorry for thee: thou art come to answer
A stony adversary, an inhuman wretch
5 Uncapable of pity, void and empty
From any dram of mercy.

Antonio   I have heard,
Your grace hath ta'en great pains to qualify
His rigorous course; but since he stands obdurate,
And that no lawful means can carry me
10 Out of his envy's reach, I do oppose
My patience to his fury, and am armed
To suffer with a quietness of spirit
The very tyranny and rage of his.

Duke   Go one, and call the Jew into the court.

15 **Solanio**   He is ready at the door, he comes, my lord.

Duke   Make room, and let him stand before our face.

[*Enter* **Shylock**]

Shylock, the world thinks, and I think so too,
That thou but leadest this fashion of thy malice
To the last hour of act, and then 'tis thought

Act four

Scene 1

A court of law in Venice. **Antonio** *enters between two guards, followed by* **Bassanio, Gratiano, Solanio, Officers** *and* **Clerks,** *and finally the* **Duke.**

Duke Well, is Antonio here?

Antonio Ready, Your Honor.

Duke I am sorry for you. You have come to answer a hard-hearted adversary: an inhuman wretch incapable of pity, totally devoid of so much as a drop of mercy.

Antonio I know Your Grace has tried hard to persuade him toward compromise. But he is obstinate, and there is no lawful way to avoid his revenge. I shall meet his fury with patience. I'm ready to submit to his violence and rage.

Duke Go, someone, and call the Jew into the court.

Solanio He is ready at the door. He's coming, my lord.

Duke Make way for him, and let him stand before me.

[*The crowd parts and* **Shylock** *stands before the* **Duke,** *bowing low*]

Shylock, everyone thinks – and I think so too – that you only intend to keep up this malice till the last minute. Then it's

20 Thou'lt show thy mercy and remorse more strange
    Than is thy strange apparent cruelty;
    And where thou now exacts the penalty,
    Which is a pound of this poor merchant's flesh,
    Thou wilt not only loose the forfeiture,
25 But touched with human gentleness and love,
    Forgive a moiety of the principal;
    Glancing an eye of pity on his losses,
    That have of late so huddled on his back;
    Enow to press a royal merchant down,
30 And pluck commiseration of his state
    From brassy bosoms and rough hearts of flint,
    From stubborn Turks and Tartars, never trained
    To offices of tender courtesy.
    We all expect a gentle answer, Jew.

35 **Shylock** I have possessed your grace of what I purpose,
    And by our holy Sabbath have I sworn
    To have the due and forfeit of my bond:
    If you deny it, let the danger light
    Upon your charter and your city's freedom!
40 You'll ask my why I rather choose to have
    A weight of carrion flesh than to receive
    Three thousand ducats: I'll not answer that!
    But say it is my humour: is it answered?
    What if my house be troubled with a rat,
45 And I be pleased to give ten thousand ducats
    To have it baned? what, are you answered yet?
    Some men there are love not a gaping pig,
    Some that are mad if they behold a cat,
    And others when the bag-pipe sings i'th' nose
50 Cannot contain their urine: for affection,
    Mistress of passion, sways it to the mood
    Of what it likes or loathes. Now, for your answer:
    As there is no firm reason to be rendred,

thought you'll show mercy and remorse more strange than
this strange apparent cruelty. And whereas you now demand
the penalty, which is one pound of this poor merchant's flesh,
you will not only forgo the forfeit, but touched with human
gentleness and love, you will forgive part of the original debt,
having pity because of the losses that have recently fallen so
heavily on him. Such losses would cripple a royal merchant
and touch the stoniest bosoms, the hardest hearts – even
those of stubborn Turks and Tartars – men unaccustomed to
tender courtesies. [*He pauses*] We all expect a gentle answer,
Jew.

Shylock   Your Grace knows my intentions. I have sworn by our
holy Sabbath to have payment in full for default on my bond. If
you deny this, your city's constitution is threatened. You will
ask me why I prefer to have a lump of dead flesh rather than
three thousand ducats. I'll not answer that! Just say it is my
whim. Is that answer enough? What if I'm troubled with a rat at
home, and I choose to give a thousand ducats to have it
poisoned? Well, have you got your answer? Some men can't
stand seeing a pig's head on a platter. Some go mad if they
see a cat. Others wet themselves when they hear the
bagpipes. For our natural inclination, a powerful emotion,
influences us to like or to despise. Now for your answer. As

Why he cannot abide a gaping pig;
55   Why he, a harmless necessary cat;
Why he, a woollen bag-pipe, but of force
Must yield to such inevitable shame,
As to offend, himself being offended;
So can I give no reason, nor I will not,
60   More than a lodged hate and a certain loathing
I bear Antonio, that I follow thus
A losing suit against him! Are you answered?

Bassanio   This is no answer, thou unfeeling man,
To excuse the current of thy cruelty!

65 **Shylock**   I am not bound to please thee with my answers!

Bassanio   Do all men kill the things they do not love?

Shylock   Hates any man the thing he would not kill?

Bassanio   Every offence is not a hate at first!

Shylock   What, wouldst thou have a serpent sting thee twice?

70 **Antonio**   I pray you, think you question with the Jew:
You may as well go stand upon the beach
And bid the main flood bate his usual height;
You may as well use question with the wolf
Why he hath made the ewe bleat with the lamb;
75   You may as well forbid the mountain pines
To wag their high tops and to make no noise
When they are fretten with the gusts of heaven;
You may as well do any thing most hard,
As seek to soften that – than which what's harder? –
80   His Jewish heart. Therefore, I do beseech you,
Make no more offers, use no farther means,
But with all brief and plain conveniency
Let me have judgement and the Jew his will!

Bassanio   For thy three thousand ducats here is six.

there is no good reason why this man can't abide a pig's head, or that man a harmless, useful cat, or this other a woollen bagpipe without shamefully losing self-control to his own and others' embarrassment, offending as he has been offended, so I can't and won't give any reason, apart from a firm hatred and a certain loathing that I have for Antonio, for pursuing a losing battle with him. Have you your answer?

Bassanio   This is not an answer, you callous man, to make excuses for your cruelty!

Shylock   I am not obliged to please you with my answers!

Bassanio   Do all men kill the things they do not love?

Shylock   Wouldn't any man want to kill the thing he hates?

Bassanio   Every offense does not cause hate, at first.

Shylock   What, would you let a serpent sting you twice?

Antonio   [*intervening*] Steady now, remember you are debating with the Jew. You might as well stand on the seashore and bid the tide not to reach its usual height, or ask the wolf why he has made the ewe cry for its lamb. You might as well forbid the mountain pine trees to sway, or make a noise, when they are buffeted by the winds. Anything equally hard you might as well attempt to do, as try to soften that hardest thing of all – his Jewish heart. Therefore, I beg you make no more objections, try no other ways, but as soon as conveniently possible, let me know the court's verdict, and let the Jew have his will.

Bassanio   For your three thousand ducats here is six!

85 **Shylock**   If every ducat in six thousand ducats
        Were in six parts and every part a ducat,
        I would not draw them: I would have my bond!

Duke   How shalt thou hope for mercy, rend'ring none?

Shylock   What judgements shall I dread, doing no wrong?
90   You have among you many a purchased slave,
        Which, like your asses and your dogs and mules,
        You use in abject and in slavish parts,
        Because you bought them: shall I say to you
        'Let them be free, marry them to your heirs?
95   Why sweat they under burthens? let their beds
        Be made as soft as yours, and let their palates
        Be seasoned with such viands?' You will answer,
        'The slaves are ours.' So do I answer you:
        The pound of flesh which I demand of him
100   Is dearly bought, 'tis mine, and I will have it:
        If you deny me, fie upon your law!
        There is no force in the decrees of Venice!
        I stand for judgement. Answer: shall I have it?

Duke   Upon my power I may dismiss this court,
105   Unless Bellario, a learned doctor,
        Whom I have sent for to determine this,
        Come here today.

Solanio   My lord, here stays without
        A messenger with letters from the doctor,
        New come from Padua.

110 **Duke**   Bring us the letters; call the messenger.

Bassanio   Good cheer, Antonio! what man, courage yet:
        The Jew shall have my flesh, blood, bones, and all,
        Ere thou shalt lose for me one drop of blood.

Shylock If every ducat in your six thousand ducats had six parts and every part were a ducat, I would not take the money. I want my bond!

Duke How can you hope for mercy, giving none yourself?

Shylock What judgment should I dread, having done no wrong? There are those among you who have purchased slaves. Like your asses, your dogs and your mules, you use them for wretched and servile jobs, because you bought them. Shall I say to you: "Let them go free. Marry them to your heirs? Why do they sweat carrying burdens? Let their beds be as soft as yours and their food be as choice?" You will reply: "The slaves are ours." I answer you likewise. The pound of flesh which I demand from him was expensive to buy. It's mine, and I will have it! If you deny it to me, I scorn your laws! The decrees of Venice have no force! I insist on justice. Answer: shall I have it?

Duke I have the power to dismiss this court, unless Bellario, a learned Doctor of Law, whom I have sent for to resolve this case, comes here today.

Solanio My lord, a messenger who has just arrived from Padua, is waiting outside with letters from the doctor.

Duke Bring me the letters. Call in the messenger.

Bassanio Cheer up, Antonio! What, man, be brave! The Jew shall have my flesh, blood, bones and all before you shall lose one drop of blood for me.

[**Shylock** *takes out a knife and begins to whet it on the soles of his leather shoes*]

Act four   Scene 1

Antonio   I am a tainted wether of the flock,
115   Meetest for death. The weakest kind of fruit
Drops earliest to the ground, and so let me;
You cannot better be employed, Bassanio,
Than to live still, and write mine epitaph.

[*Enter* **Nerissa**]

Duke   Came you from Padua, from Bellario?

120 **Nerissa**   From both, my lord. Bellario greets your grace.

[*She presents a letter*]

Bassanio   Why dost thou whet thy knife so earnestly?

Shylock   To cut the forfeiture from that bankrupt there.

Gratiano   Not on thy sole, but on thy soul, harsh Jew,
Thou mak'st thy knife keen: but no metal can,
125   No, not the hangman's axe, bear half the keenness
Of thy sharp envy: can no prayers pierce thee?

Shylock   No, none that thou hast wit enough to make.

Gratiano   O, be thou damned, inexorable dog,
And for thy life let justice be accused!
130   Thou almost mak'st me waver in my faith,
To hold opinion with Pythagoras
That souls of animals infuse themselves
Into the trunks of men: thy currish spirit
Governed a wolf, who hanged for human slaughter,
135   Even from the gallows did his fell soul fleet,
And whilst thou layest in thy unhallowed dam,
Infused itself in thee; for thy desires
Are wolvish, bloody, starved, and ravenous.

Antonio   I am the lame lamb of the flock: most apt for death. The feeblest fruit drops earliest to the ground, and so let me. You cannot use your time better, Bassanio, than to stay alive and write my epitaph.

[**Nerissa** *enters, dressed as a lawyer's clerk*]

Duke   Did you come from Padua? From Bellario?

Nerisa   [*bowing*] From both, my lord. Bellario sends his greeting to Your Grace. [*She presents a letter, which the* **Duke** *reads*]

Bassanio   [*to* **Shylock**] Why are you sharpening your knife so earnestly?

Shylock   To cut the forfeiture from that bankrupt there.

Gratiano   You are sharpening your knife not on your shoe's sole, harsh Jew, but on your immortal soul. But no metal, not even the executioner's axe, is half as keen as your sharp envy. Can no prayers touch you?

Shylock   No. None that you have brains to make.

Gratiano   Damn you, you unyielding dog! Justice is to blame for letting you live. I almost doubt my faith and share Pythagoras's theory that the bodies of animals inhabit men. Your cur-like spirit comes from a wolf whose soul, when he was hanged for killing humans, fled into the womb of your damned mother, and mingled itself in you! Your desires are wolfish, bloody, mean and ravenous!

Shylock   Till thou canst rail the seal from off my bond,
140   Thou but offend'st thy lungs to speak so loud:
Repair thy wit, good youth, or it will fall
To cureless ruin. I stand here for law.

Duke   This letter from Bellario doth commend
A young and learned doctor to our court:
Where is he?

145 **Nerissa**   He attendeth here hard by
To know your answer, whether you'll admit him.

Duke   With all my heart: some three or four of you
Go give him courteous conduct to this place.
Meantime, the court shall hear Bellario's letter.

150   'Your grace shall understand that at the receipt of your letter I
am very sick, but in the instant that your messenger came, in
loving visitation was with me a young doctor of Rome, his
name is Balthazar. I acquainted him with the cause in
controversy between the Jew and Antonio the merchant; we
155   turned o'er many books together; he is furnished with my
opinion, which bettered with his own learning, the greatness
whereof I cannot enough commend, comes with him at my
importunity to fill up your grace's request in my stead. I
beseech you, let his lack of years be no impediment to let him
160   lack a reverend estimation, for I never knew so young a body
with so old a head. I leave him to your gracious acceptance,
whose trial shall better publish his commendation.'

You hear the learned Bellario, what he writes.

[*Enter* **Portia**]

And here, I take it, is the doctor come.
165   Give me your hand. Come you from old Bellario?

Portia   I did, my lord.

Shylock [*scorning him*] Till you can rant the seal from off my bond, you are merely damaging your lungs in shouting so loud. Mend your wit, young man, or it will collapse in ruins, beyond repair! I stand here for justice.

Duke This letter from Bellario recommends to our court a young and learned doctor: where is he?

Nerissa He is waiting nearby to know your answer – whether you will admit him.

Duke With all my heart. Three or four of you go and escort him courteously to this place. [**Attendants** *leave*] Meanwhile, the court shall hear Bellario's letter: [*He reads*]

"Your Grace, when your letter arrived, I was very sick. But when your messenger came, there was with me a young doctor of law from Rome – Balthazar – paying a friendly visit. I told him of the lawsuit between the Jew and Antonio the merchant. We consulted many books together. I have asked him to come in my place, in response to Your Grace's invitation. He knows my opinion. It has the benefit of his own great learning, of which I cannot speak too highly. I beg you not to underestimate him on account of his youth. I never knew so young a body to have so old a head. I trust you will accept him. His performance will speak for itself." [*He looks up*]

You hear what the learned Bellario has written.

[**Portia** *enters, dressed as a lawyer, carrying a lawbook*]

And here, I take it, is the doctor himself. [*He greets her*] Give me your hand. [*They shake*] You've come from old Bellario?

Portia I have, my lord.

Duke   You are welcome. Take your place.
Are you acquainted with the difference
That holds this present question in the court?

170 **Portia**   I am informed thoroughly of the cause.
Which is the merchant here, and which the Jew?

Duke   Antonio and old Shylock both stand forth.

Portia   Is your name Shylock?

Shylock   Shylock is my name.

Portia   Of a strange nature is the suit you follow,
175   Yet in such rule that the Venetian law
Cannot impugn you as you do proceed.
You stand within his danger, do you not?

Antonio   Ay, so he says.

Portia   Do you confess the bond?

Antonio   I do.

Portia   Then must the Jew be merciful

180 **Shylock**   On what compulsion must I? tell me that.

Portia   The quality of mercy is not strained,
It droppeth as the gentle rain from heaven
Upon the place beneath. It is twice blessed:
It blesseth him that gives, and him that takes.
185   'Tis mightiest in the mightiest, it becomes
The thronèd monarch better than his crown:
His sceptre shows the force of temporal power,
The attribute to awe and majesty,
Wherein doth sit the dread and fear of kings:
190   But mercy is above this sceptred sway,
It is enthroned in the hearts of kings,
It is an attribute to God himself;
And earthly power doth then show likest God's,

Duke You are welcome. Take your place. [*A court usher guides* **Portia** *to a desk near the* **Duke**] Are you acquainted with the dispute before the court?

Portia I am well acquainted with the case. Which is the merchant, and which the Jew?

Duke Antonio and Shylock, stand up.

[*They step forward and bow before the* **Duke**]

Portia Is your name Shylock?

Shylock Shylock is my name.

Portia Your case is an unusual one. But it is sufficiently sound that Venetian laws cannot prevent you from proceeding. [*To* **Antonio**] You stand in some danger from him, do you not?

Antonio Yes, so he says.

Portia Do you admit to the bond?

Antonio I do.

Portia Then the Jew must be merciful.

Shylock By what force *must* I? Tell me that!

Portia The quality of mercy is not strained. It drops like the gentle rain from heaven upon the place beneath. It is twice blessed: It blesses him who gives and him who takes. It is mightiest when rendered by the mighty. It is a more important symbol than the king's crown. His scepter shows the force of earthly power, the symbol of his awe and majesty, the reason kings are held in dread and fear. But mercy is above this sceptered rule. It is enthroned in the hearts of kings. It is an attribute to God himself. Earthly power is nearest to God's

When mercy seasons justice. Therefore, Jew,
195   Though justice be thy plea, consider this,
That in the course of justice none of us
Should see salvation: we do pray for mercy,
And that same prayer doth teach us all to render
The deeds of mercy. I have spoke thus much,
200   To mitigate the justice of thy plea,
Which if thou follow, this strict court of Venice
Must needs give sentence 'gainst the merchant there.

Shylock   My deeds upon my head! I crave the law,
The penalty and forfeit of my bond.

205 **Portia**   Is he not able to discharge the money?

Bassanio   Yes, here I tender it for him in the court,
Yea, twice the sum. If that will not suffice,
I will be bound to pay it ten times o'er,
On forfeit of my hands, my head, my heart.
210   If this will not suffice, it must appear
That malice bears down truth. And I beseech you,
Wrest once the law to your authority –
To do a great right, do a little wrong,
And curb this cruel devil of his will.

215 **Portia**   It must not be, there is no power in Venice
Can alter a decree established:
'Twill be recorded for a precedent,
And many an error by the same example
Will rush into the state. It cannot be.

Shylock   A Daniel come to judgement: yea, a Daniel!
O wise young judge, how I do honour thee!

Portia   I pray you, let me look upon the bond.

220 **Shylock**   Here 'tis, most reverend doctor, here it is.

Portia   Shylock, there's thrice thy money offered thee.

when justice is tempered by mercy. Therefore, Jew, though you claim justice for yourself, consider this. None of us could expect salvation if justice alone prevailed. So we pray for mercy. And in seeking it ourselves, we learn to be merciful to others. I have said all this to qualify the justice of your plea. If you insist on it, then this strict Venetian court has no choice but to pronounce sentence against the merchant there.

Shylock I'll answer for my own behavior! I'm asking for my rights: the penalty and the forfeit, according to my bond!

Portia Can he not settle with you?

Bassanio Yes, I offer it to him now in court, indeed twice the sum. If that's not enough, I'll willingly be bound over to pay ten times the sum, on forfeit of my hands, my head or my heart. If this is not enough, malice is obscuring truth. [*He kneels before* **Portia** *in an attitude of prayer*] I beg you: twist the law your way. To do a great right, do a little wrong, and prevent this cruel devil having his will!

Portia That's impossible. There is no power in Venice that can overrule a lawful decree. It would create a precedent and thereby lead to other irregularities in the state. It cannot be.

Shylock [*delighted*] A Daniel come to give justice, yes, a Daniel! [*He kisses the hem of her robe*] Oh, wise young judge! How I honor you!

Portia Permit me to read the bond.

Shylock [*all haste to hand it over*] Here it is, most reverend doctor, here it is!

Portia [*accepting the document but not reading it yet*] Shylock, you have been offered three times the money . . .

225 **Shylock**   An oath, an oath, I have an oath in heaven.
Shall I lay perjury upon my soul?
No, not for Venice.

Portia   Why this bond is forfeit,
And lawfully by this the Jew may claim
A pound of flesh, to be by him cut off
230 Nearest the merchant's heart. Be merciful,
Take thrice thy money, bid me tear the bond.

Shylock   When it is paid according to the tenour.
It doth appear you are a worthy judge,
You know the law, your exposition
235 Hath been most sound: I charge you by the law,
Whereof you are a well-deserving pillar,
Proceed to judgement: by my soul I swear,
There is no power in the tongue of man
To alter me. I stay here on my bond.

240 **Antonio**   Most heartily I do beseech the court
To give the judgement.

Portia   Why then, thus it is.
You must prepare your bosom for his knife.

Shylock   O noble judge! O excellent young man!

Portia   For the intent and purpose of the law
245 Hath full relation to the penalty,
Which here appeareth due upon the bond.

Shylock   'Tis very true: O wise and upright judge!
How much more elder art thou than thy looks!

Portia   Therefore, lay bare your bosom.

Shylock   Ay, his breast,
250 So says the bond, doth it not, noble judge?
'Nearest his heart,' those are the very words.

Shylock   My oath! My oath! I have vowed an oath to heaven! Shall my soul be guilty of perjury? No, not for Venice itself.

Portia   [*scanning the bond*] Well, this bond is forfeit. By this, the Jew may lawfully claim a pound of flesh, to be cut out by him nearest to the merchant's heart. [*To* **Shylock**] Be merciful. Take three times your money. Tell me to tear up the bond.

Shylock   Only when it is paid according to the agreement. You seem to be a worthy judge. You know the law. Your interpretation was very sound. I demand in the name of the law, of which you are a well-deserving pillar, proceed to judgment. I swear upon my soul that no man has the power to persuade me otherwise. I'll have my bond!

Antonio   Wholeheartedly I beg the court to proceed to judgment.

Portia   Well, then. Here it is. You must prepare your breast for the knife.

Shylock   Oh, noble judge! Oh, excellent young man!

Portia   The object of the law is to support the penalty, which [*indicating the bond*] here seems due, according to the bond.

Shylock   That's very true. Oh, wise and upright judge! How much older are you than you look!

Portia   [*to* **Antonio**] Therefore, lay bare your breast.

Shylock   Yes, his chest. That's what the bond says, does it not, noble judge? "Nearest his heart." Those are the very words.

Portia   It is so. Are there balance here, to weigh
The flesh?

Shylock   I have them ready.

Portia   Have by some surgeon, Shylock, on your charge,
255   To stop his wounds, lest he do bleed to death.

Shylock   Is it so nominated in the bond?

Portia   It is not so expressed, but what of that?
'Twere good you do so much for charity.

Shylock   I cannot find it, 'tis not in the bond.

260 **Portia**   You merchant, have you any thing to say?

Antonio   But little; I am armed and well prepared.
Give me your hand Bassanio, fare you well!
Grieve not that I am fall'n to this for you;
For herein Fortune shows herself more kind
265   Than is her custom: it is still her use,
To let the wretched man outlive his wealth,
To view with hollow eye and wrinkled brow
An age of poverty; from which ling'ring penance
Of such misery doth she cut me off.
270   Commend me to your honourable wife,
Tell her the process of Antonio's end,
Say how I loved you, speak me fair in death;
And when the tale is told, bid her be judge
Whether Bassanio had not once a love.
275   Repent but you that you shall lose your friend,
And he repents not, that he pays your debt;
For if the Jew do cut but deep enough,
I'll pay it instantly with all my heart.

Bassanio   Antonio, I am married to a wife
280   Which is as dear to me as life itself,
But life itself, my wife, and all the world,
Are not with me esteemed above thy life:
I would lose all, ay, sacrifice them all
Here to this devil, to deliver you.

Portia That's so. Have we scales here, to weigh the flesh?

Shylock I have them ready. [*He opens his cloak to reveal them*]

Portia Order a doctor to stand by, Shylock, to stop his wounds, in case he bleeds to death.

Shylock Does it specify that in the bond? [*He takes up the document again and reads it closely*]

Portia It isn't spelled out, but what of that? You'd do that much out of charity.

Shylock I can't find it. It isn't in the bond. [*He hands it back*]

Portia You, merchant. Have you anything to say?

Antonio Very little. I have braced myself and I'm well prepared. Give me your hand, Bassanio. Farewell! Don't grieve because I've come to this for you. In my case, Fortune is kinder than usual. Frequently she lets the wretched man outlive his money, to endure with sunken eye and wrinkled brow an old age of abject poverty. She's spared me that long-drawn-out misery. [*They embrace*] My regards to your dear wife. Tell her how Antonio came to die. Tell her I loved you. Speak well of me in death. And when the tale is told, ask her to judge whether or not Bassanio was loved. Only regret that you will lose your friend. He has no regret in paying what you owe. If the Jew cuts deep enough, I'll pay it instantly, with all my heart!

Bassanio Antonio, I am married to a wife who is as dear to me as life itself. But life itself, my wife and all the world are not to me more precious than your life. I would lose them all, yes, sacrifice them all, to this devil here [*pointing to* **Shylock**] to rescue you.

285 **Portia**   Your wife would give you little thanks for that,
If she were by, to hear you make the offer.

Gratiano   I have a wife, whom, I protest, I love:
I would she were in heaven, so she could
Entreat some power to change this currish Jew.

290 **Nerissa**   'Tis well you offer it behind her back:
The wish would make else an unquiet house.

Shylock   These be the Christian husbands! I have a daughter –
Would any of the stock of Barabas
Had been her husband, rather than a Christian.
295 We trifle time, I pray thee pursue sentence.

Portia   A pound of that same merchant's flesh is thine,
The court awards it, and the law doth give it.

Shylock   Most rightful judge!

Portia   And you must cut this flesh from off his breast:
300 The law allows it, and the court awards it.

Shylock   Most learned judge! A sentence! Come prepare!

Portia   Tarry a little: there is something else.
This bond doth give thee here no jot of blood –
The words expressly are 'a pound of flesh';
305 Take then thy bond, take then thy pound of flesh,
But in the cutting it, if thou dost shed
One drop of Christian blood, thy lands and goods
Are by the laws of Venice confiscate
Unto the state of Venice.

310 **Gratiano**   O upright judge! Mark, Jew! O learned judge!

Shylock   Is that the law!

Portia   Thyself shalt see the act:
For, as thou urgest justice, be assured
Thou shalt have justice more than thou desir'st.

Portia Your wife would give you little thanks if she were here to hear you make that offer!

Gratiano I have a wife whom I swear I love. I wish she were in heaven so she could plead with someone in authority there to change this cur of a Jew!

Nerissa It's as well you offer that behind her back, otherwise you'd have an unhappy wife!

Shylock [*aside*] So much for Christian husbands! I have a daughter. I'd rather she married one of that villain Barabbas's line than a Christian! [*Aloud*] We're wasting time. Proceed to sentence, I beg of you.

Portia A pound of this merchant's flesh is yours. The court awards it. The law permits it.

Shylock Most rightful judge!

Portia And you must cut this flesh from his breast. The law allows it, and the court awards it.

Shylock Most learned judge! A sentence! [*He moves with knife drawn toward* **Antonio**] Come, prepare!

Portia Wait a moment. There is something else. This bond [*holding it up*] does not give you one drop of blood. The words expressly are [*she reads*] "a pound of flesh." So take your bond. Take your pound of flesh. But if, in cutting it, you shed one drop of Christian blood, your lands and goods, under the laws of Venice, will be confiscated to the state of Venice.

Gratiano [*understanding dawns*] Oh, upright judge! Take heed, Jew! Oh, learned judge!

Shylock [*appalled*] Is that the law?

Portia [*opening the lawbook*] You can see the Act for yourself. You pressed for justice. Be assured you shall have more justice than you want.

Gratiano   O learned judge! Mark, Jew! A learned judge!

315 **Shylock**   I take this offer then; pay the bond thrice,
And let the Christian go.

Bassanio   Here is the money.

Portia   Soft!
The Jew shall have all justice; soft, no haste:
He shall have nothing but the penalty.

Gratiano   O Jew! an upright judge, a learned judge!

320 **Portia**   Therefore, prepare thee to cut off the flesh.
Shed thou no blood, nor cut thou less nor more
But just a pound of flesh: if thou tak'st more
Or less than a just pound, be it but so much
As makes it light or heavy in the substance,
325 Or the division of the twentieth part
Of one poor scruple, nay, if the scale do turn
But in the estimation of a hair,
Thou diest and all thy goods are confiscate.

Gratiano   A second Daniel, a Daniel, Jew!
330 Now, infidel, I have you on the hip.

Portia   Why doth the Jew pause? take thy forfeiture.

Shylock   Give me my principal, and let me go.

Bassanio   I have it ready for thee; here it is.

Portia   He hath refused it in the open court,
335 He shall have merely justice and his bond.

Gratiano   A Daniel, still say I, a second Daniel!
I thank thee Jew, for teaching me that word.

Shylock   Shall I not have barely my principal?

Portia   Thou shalt have nothing but the forfeiture
340 To be so taken at thy peril, Jew.

Gratiano [*pressing the point*] Oh, learned judge! Take heed, Jew! A learned judge!

Shylock   I accept the offer then. Pay three times the bond and let the Christian go.

Bassanio   Here's the money.

Portia [*raising her hand*] Gently now. The Jew shall have complete justice. Gently now. No haste. He shall have nothing other than the penalty.

Gratiano   Oh, Jew! An upright judge, a learned judge!

Portia   Therefore, prépare to cut off the flesh. Shed no blood. And cut neither more nor less than exactly one pound of flesh. If you take more or less than a pound, even if only by enough to make the piece light or heavy by as little as one twentieth of a minute fraction – no, if the scale turns by so little as a hair – then you shall die and all your property will be confiscated.

Gratiano   He's a second Daniel! A Daniel, Jew! Now, you infidel, I've got you squirming!

Portia   Why does the Jew pause? Take your forfeit.

Shylock [*thwarted*] Give me my money back, and let me go.

Bassanio   I have it ready for you. Here it is.

Portia   He has refused it in open court. He shall have strict justice, according to his bond.

Gratiano   A Daniel, still say I, a second Daniel! Thank you, Jew, for teaching me that word.

Shylock [*aghast*] Shall I not have my money back, even?

Portia   You shall have nothing but the forfeit, and that to be taken at your peril, Jew.

Shylock   Why then the devil give him good of it!
I'll stay no longer question.

Portia   Tarry, Jew.
The law hath yet another hold on you.
It is enacted in the laws of Venice,
345   If it be proved against an alien,
That by direct or indirect attempts
He seek the life of any citizen,
The party 'gainst the which he doth contrive
Shall seize one half his goods, the other half
350   Comes to the privy coffer of the state,
And the offender's life lies in the mercy
Of the duke only, 'gainst all other voice.
In which predicament, I say, thou stand'st:
For it appears by manifest proceeding,
355   That indirectly and directly too
Thou hast contrived against the very life
Of the defendant; and thou hast incurred
The danger formerly by me rehearsed.
Down, therefore, and beg mercy of the duke.

360   **Gratiano**   Beg that thou mayst have leave to hang thyself,
And yet thy wealth being forfeit to the state,
Thou hast not left the value of a cord,
Therefore thou must be hanged at the state's charge.

Duke   That thou shalt see the difference of our spirit,
365   I pardon thee thy life before thou ask it:
For half thy wealth, it is Antonio's:
The other half comes to the general state,
Which humbleness may drive unto a fine.

Portia   Ay, for the state, not for Antonio.

370   **Shylock**   Nay, take my life and all, pardon not that.
You take my house, when you take the prop

Shylock   Well, then, may the devil give him joy of it! I'll tolerate no more of this. [*He turns to go*]

Portia   Wait a moment, Jew. The law has yet another hold over you. [*She consults her lawbook again*] It is a law of Venice that if it is proved against an alien that by direct or indirect means he seeks the life of any citizen, the person against whom he plots is entitled to seize one half of his possessions. The other half goes to the state treasury. The life of the offender is at the duke's sole discretion. [*She closes the book*] I say you stand in that predicament. It is obvious from your actions that indirectly, and directly too, you have plotted against the life of the defendant: you are indeed in danger of the death penalty, as I have explained. Down on your knees, therefore, and beg the duke for mercy.

Gratiano   Beg the right to hang yourself! But seeing your fortune is forfeit to the state, you couldn't afford the rope. You'll have to be hanged at the state's expense!

Duke   So that you may see the difference in our attitudes, I pardon your life before you ask for it. Half your wealth goes to Antonio: the other half goes to the state. Contrition on your part could turn this to a fine.

Portia   Yes, the state's half, not Antonio's.

Shylock   [*a broken man*] No, take my life as well! Don't pardon that! You take my house, when you remove my source of

That doth sustain my house: you take my life,
When you do take the means whereby I live.

Portia   What mercy can you render him, Antonio?

375 **Gratiano**   A halter gratis – nothing else, for God's sake.

Antonio   So please my lord the duke and all the court
To quit the fine for one half of his goods,
I am content; so he will let me have
The other half in use, to render it
380 Upon his death unto the gentleman
That lately stole his daughter;
Two things provided more, that, for this favour,
He presently become a Christian;
The other, that he do record a gift,
385 Here in the court, of all he dies possessed,
Unto his son Lorenzo and his daughter.

Duke   He shall do this, or else I do recant
The pardon that I late pronounced here.

Portia   Art thou contented, Jew? what dost thou say?

Shylock   I am content.

390 **Portia**   Clerk, draw a deed of gift.

Shylock   I pray you give me leave to go from hence,
I am not well, send the deed after me,
And I will sign it.

Duke   Get thee gone, but do it.

Gratiano   In christ'ning shalt thou have two godfathers –
395 Had I been judge, thou shouldst have had ten more,
To bring thee to the gallows, not to the font.

[*Exit* **Shylock**]

income. You take my life when you take away the means
whereby I earn a living.

Portia   Can you offer him any mercy, Antonio?

Gratiano   A noose, free of charge. For God's sake, nothing else!

Antonio   I would be satisfied if his lordship the duke, and the
court, were willing to waive the fine which replaced the
confiscation of half his fortune, provided I can have the other
half in trust during his lifetime. Thereafter, I'll return it to the
gentleman who recently eloped with his daughter. Two
conditions more. One: in return for this clemency, he shall
become a Christian immediately. Two: that he makes a will
here in court, leaving all he possesses at his death to his
son-in-law Lorenzo and his daughter.

Duke   This he will do, or I'll withdraw the pardon I have just
pronounced!

Portia   Do you agree, Jew? What do you say?

Shylock   [*a shattered man*] I agree.

Portia   [*to* **Nerissa**] Clerk, draw up a deed of gift.

Shylock   Please, grant me permission to leave here. I am not
well. Send the will after me, and I will sign it.

Duke   You may leave, but see you do it!

Gratiano   When you are christened, you'll have two
godfathers. If I'd been the judge, you'd have had ten more, to
take you to the gallows, not the font!

[**Shylock** *staggers out amidst jeers*]

Duke   Sir, I entreat you home with me to dinner.

Portia   I humbly do desire your grace of pardon,
I must away this night toward Padua,
400   And it is meet I presently set forth.

Duke   I am sorry that your leisure serves you not.
Antonio, gratify this gentleman,
For in my mind you are much bound to him.

[*Exeunt the* **Duke** *and his train*]

Bassanio   Most worthy gentleman, I and my friend
405   Have by your wisdom been this day acquitted
Of grievous penalties, in lieu whereof,
Three thousand ducats, due unto the Jew,
We freely cope your courteous pains withal.

Antonio   And stand indebted, over and above,
410   In love and service to you evermore.

Portia   He is well paid that is well satisfied,
And I, delivering you, am satisfied,
And therein do account myself well paid.
My mind was never yet more mercenary.
415   I pray you, know me when we meet again:
I wish you well, and so I take my leave.

Bassanio   Dear sir, of force I must attempt you further.
Take some remembrance of us, as a tribute,
Not as fee: grant me two things, I pray you,
420   Not to deny me, and to pardon me.

Portia   You press me far, and therefore I will yield.
Give me your gloves, I'll wear them for your sake.
And, for your love, I'll take this ring from you:
Do not draw back your hand; I'll take no more,
425   And you in love shall not deny me this?

Duke [*rising, to* **Portia**] Sir, I hope you will dine with me at home?

Portia I humbly beg Your Grace's pardon. I must leave tonight for Padua, and the sooner I set off the better.

Duke I'm sorry you cannot spare the time. [*To* **Antonio**] Antonio, reward this gentleman. You are greatly indebted to him, I think.

[*The* **Duke** *and his* **Attendants** *depart*]

Bassanio [*to* **Portia**] My good sir, I and my friend have been spared the most grievous of penalties today as a result of your wise counsel. We gladly recompense your efforts with the three thousand ducats due to the Jew.

Antonio In love and gratitude, we shall be indebted to you far more than that, forevermore.

Portia [*refusing the money*] To be well satisfied is to be well paid. In rescuing you, I'm satisfied. And therefore I regard myself well paid. I think of money no more than that. [*She bows and passes them*] Pray, remember me when we meet again. I wish you well and say goodbye to you. [*She makes to leave*]

Bassanio [*following her anxiously*] Dear sir, I really must press you again. Take some souvenir of us, as a gesture, not as a fee. Grant me two things, if you would: don't say no, and excuse my persistence.

Portia [*stopping at the door*] You press me hard, and therefore I'll give in. Give me your gloves. I'll wear them to oblige you. [**Bassanio** *removes them willingly*] And, in token of your love, I'll take this ring from you. [**Bassanio** *withdraws his hand sharply*] Don't draw back your hand. I'll take no more from you. You surely won't deny me this?

Bassanio   This ring, good sir – alas, it is a trifle!
I will not shame myself to give you this.

Portia   I will have nothing else but only this;
And now, methinks, I have a mind to it.

430 **Bassanio**   There's more depends on this than on the value.
The dearest ring in Venice will I give you,
And find it out by proclamation,
Only this, I pray you. pardon me.

Portia   I see, sir, you are liberal in offers.
435   You taught me first to beg, and now, methinks,
You teach me how a beggar should be answered.

Bassanio   Good sir, this ring was given me by my wife,
And when she put it on, she made me vow
That I should neither sell nor give nor lose it.

440 **Portia**   That 'scuse serves many men to save their gifts.
And if your wife be not a mad-woman,
And know how well I have deserved this ring,
She would not hold out enemy for ever,
For giving it to me. Well, peace be with you!

[*Exeunt* **Portia** *and* **Nerissa**]

445 **Antonio**   My Lord Bassanio, let him have the ring.
Let his deservings and my love withal
Be valued 'gainst your wife's commandment.

Bassanio   Go, Gratiano, run and overtake him,
Give him the ring; and bring him if thou canst
450   Unto Antonio's house; away, make haste.

[*Exit* **Gratiano**]

Come, you and I will thither presently,

Bassanio [*confused*] This ring, dear sir – alas, it's worthless. I wouldn't shame myself by giving it to you.

Portia   [*stiffly*] I will have nothing other than this. I've taken a fancy to it.

Bassanio   This ring has more importance than its value. I'll give you the most expensive ring in Venice and advertise for it. With respect, you must pardon me on this one.

Portia   I see, sir, you are generous with your offers. First you taught me how to beg. Now, it seems, you are teaching me how a beggar should be answered.

Bassanio   Good sir, this ring was given to me by my wife. When she put it on, she made me promise that I would never sell, or give, or lose it.

Portia   That's an excuse many men use to retain their gifts. And if your wife isn't a madwoman, knowing how well I deserve this ring, she won't be angry with you forever for giving it to me. Well, peace be with you!

[*She sweeps out, followed by* **Nerissa**]

Antonio   [*distressed*] Lord Bassanio, let him have the ring! Weigh his worthiness and my love against your wife's commandment.

Bassanio   [*yielding*] Run, Gratiano, catch him. Give him the ring. And if you can, bring him to Antonio's house. Go quickly!

[**Gratiano** *hurries in pursuit*]

[*to* **Antonio**] Come. You and I will go there immediately. And

> And in the morning early will we both
> Fly toward Belmont. Come, Antonio.

[Exeunt]

Scene 2

A street in Venice. Enter **Portia** *and* **Nerissa.**

Portia   Inquire the Jew's house out, give him this deed,
And let him sign it. We'll away tonight,
And be a day before our husbands home:
This deed will be well welcome to Lorenzo.

[*Enter* **Gratiano**]

5 **Gratiano**   Fair sir, you are well o'erta'en.
My Lord Bassanio, upon more advice,
Hath sent you here this ring, and doth entreat
Your company at dinner.

Portia   That cannot be:
His ring I do accept most thankfully,
10 And so I pray you tell him: furthermore,
I pray you, show my youth old Shylock's house.

Gratiano   That will I do.

Nerissa   [*Aside to* **Portia**]   Sir, I would speak with you.
I'll see if I can get my husband's ring,
Which I did make him swear to keep for ever.

early tomorrow morning we will both hurry to Belmont.
Come, Antonio.

[*They leave together*]

Scene 2

A street outside the Law Courts in Venice. **Portia** *and* **Nerissa**
enter.

Portia [*giving a paper to* **Nerissa**] Ask the way to the Jew's
house, give him this document and see he signs it. We'll leave
tonight and reach home a day before our husbands. This deed
will be very welcome to Lorenzo.

[**Gratiano** *runs breathless from the Court buildings*]

Gratiano Sir, I've caught up with you at last. My Lord Bassanio,
further advised, has sent this ring to you and requests your
company at dinner.

Portia That's not possible. I accept his ring most gratefully.
Pray tell him so. One more thing! Please show my young man
old Shylock's house.

Gratiano I'll do that.

Nerissa [*to* **Portia**] Sir, I'd like a word with you. [*She takes*
Portia *aside*] I'll see if I can get my husband's ring – the one I
made him swear to keep forever!

15 **Portia**   Thou mayst, I warrant. We shall have old swearing
        That they did give the rings away to men;
        But we'll outface them, and outswear them too.
        Away, make haste, thou know'st where I will tarry.

    Nerissa   Come, good sir, will you show me to this house?

                                           [*Exeunt*]

Portia   You can, I'm sure. They'll be sure to swear that they gave the rings away to men! But we'll stand up to them, and outswear them, too! Away, make haste. You know where I'll be waiting for you.

Nerissa   [*to* **Gratiano**] Come, sir, will you show me to his house?

[*They leave in the direction of* **Shylock**'*s house*]

Act five

Scene 1

Portia's house in Belmont. Enter **Lorenzo** *and* **Jessica**.

Lorenzo   The moon shines bright. In such a night as this,
When the sweet wind did gently kiss the trees,
And they did make no noise, in such a night
Troilus methinks mounted the Troyan walls,
5   And sighed his soul towards the Grecian tents,
Where Cressid lay that night.

Jessica   In such a night
Did Thisbe fearfully o'ertrip the dew,
And saw the lion's shadow ere himself,
And ran dismayed away.

Lorenzo   In such a night
10   Stood Dido with a willow in her hand
Upon the wild sea banks, and waft her love
To come again to Carthage.

Jessica   In such a night
Medea gathered the enchanted herbs
That did renew old Aeson.

Lorenzo   In such a night
15   Did Jessica steal from the wealthy Jew,
And with an unthrift love did run from Venice
As far as Belmont.

Jessica   In such a night
Did young Lorenzo swear he loved her well,
Stealing her soul with many vows of faith,
And ne'er a true one.

Act five

Scene 1

The garden at **Portia**'s *house in Belmont, on a moonlit night in summer.*

Lorenzo   The moon shines bright. On such a night as this, when the soft wind gently kissed the trees, and they were silent, on such a night, I think Troilus climbed the Trojan walls, and sighed soulfully toward the Grecian tents, where Cressida slept that night.

Jessica   [*taking up the theme*] On such a night, Thisbe tiptoed over the dew, and seeing the shadow of a lion, ran away distressed.

Lorenzo   [*it is a game now*] On such a night, Dido stood with a willow in her hand, on the wild sea coast, summoning her lover to return to Carthage.

Jessica   [*after the slightest of pauses*] On such a night, Medea gathered the enchanted herbs that rejuvenated old Aeson.

Lorenzo   [*reality now*] On such a night, Jessica stole away from the wealthy Jew, and with a bounteous love she ran from Venice to Belmont.

Jessica   [*teasing*] On such a night, young Lorenzo swore he truly loved her, and stole her soul with many declarations of faith. And none of them honest!

20 **Lorenzo**   In such a night
    Did pretty Jessica, like a little shrew,
    Slander her love, and he forgave it her.

   Jessica   I would out-night you, did no body come:
    But, hark, I hear the footing of a man.

    [*Enter* **Stephano**]

25 **Lorenzo**   Who comes so fast in silence of the night?

   Stephano   A friend.

   Lorenzo   A friend! what friend? your name, I pray you friend?

   Stephano   Stephano is my name, and I bring word
    My mistress will before the break of day
30 Be here at Belmont: she doth stray about
    By holy crosses, where she kneels and prays
    For happy wedlock hours.

   Lorenzo   Who comes with her?

   Stephano   None, but a holy hermit and her maid.
    I pray you, is my master yet returned?

35 **Lorenzo**   He is not, nor we have not heard from him.
    But go we in, I pray thee, Jessica,
    And ceremoniously let us prepare
    Some welcome for the mistress of the house.

    [*Enter* **Lancelot**]

   Lancelot   Sola, sola! wo ha, ho, sola, sola!

40 **Lorenzo**   Who calls?

   Lancelot   Sola! did you see Master Lorenzo? Master Lorenzo?
    sola, sola!

Lorenzo [*wincing*] On such a night did pretty Jessica (like a little shrew!) slander her lover, and he forgave her.

Jessica I'd beat you at this "night" game, if uninterrupted. But listen! I hear footsteps!

[**Stephano,** *a servant of* **Portia**'*s, runs on*]

Lorenzo Who comes running in the silence of the night?

Stephano A friend.

Lorenzo A friend? What friend? Your name, friend, if you please.

Stephano My name's Stephano. My message is that my mistress will arrive at Belmont before dawn. At every holy cross she kneels and prays for a happy married life.

Lorenzo Who's with her?

Stephano Only a holy hermit, and her maid. Has my master returned yet, may I ask?

Lorenzo He hasn't, nor have we heard from him. But let's go in, Jessica, and formally prepare a welcome for the mistress of the house.

[**Lancelot** *can be heard making bugle noises*]

Lancelot Hello there! Ta ra, ta, ta ra!

Lorenzo Who's that?

Lancelot [*still bugling*] Hello-o-o! Have you seen Master Lorenzo? [*Calling again*] Master Lorenzo! Hello-o!

Lorenzo   Leave hollaing, man: here!

Lancelot   Sola! where? where?

Lorenzo   Here!

45 **Lancelot**   Tell him, there's a post come from my master, with
his horn full of good news. My master will be here ere
morning.

[*Exit*]

Lorenzo   Sweet soul, let's in, and there expect their coming.
And yet no matter: why should we go in?
50   My friend Stephano, signify, I pray you,
Within the house, your mistress is at hand,
And bring your music forth into the air.

[*Exit* **Stephano**]

How sweet the moonlight sleeps upon this bank!
Here will we sit and let the sounds of music
55   Creep in our ears: soft stillness and the night
Become the touches of sweet harmony.
Sit, Jessica. Look how the floor of heaven
Is thick inlaid with patens of bright gold:
There's not the smallest orb which thou behold'st
60   But in his motion like an angel sings,
Still choiring to the young-eyed cherubins;
Such harmony is in immortal souls!
But whilst this muddy vesture of decay
Doth grossly close it in, we cannot hear it.

[*Enter* **Musicians**]

65   Come, ho, and wake Diana with a hymn!
With sweetest touches pierce your mistress' ear,
And draw her home with music.

Lorenzo   Stop yelling, man! I'm here.

Lancelot   Hello! Where? Where?

Lorenzo   Here!

Lancelot   Well, tell him a messenger has arrived from my master, with his postbag full of good news. My master will be here by morning.

[*He runs off*]

Lorenzo   Dearest, let's go in and wait for their arrival. And yet, why? Why should we go in? [*To* **Stephano**] Friend Stephano, please inform those inside the house that your mistress is nearby, and then bring the musicians out.

[**Stephano** *goes indoors*]

How sweetly the moonlight rests upon this bank! We'll sit here and let the sounds of music fall gently on our ears. Soft stillness and night are suited to the charms of sweet harmony. Sit, Jessica, Look how the night sky is dense with radiant jewels! Even the smallest star sings in its musical sphere like an angel in a choir, chorusing before the keen-eyed cherubim. Immortal souls can hear such harmonies, but we cannot hear, enclosed as we are within our coarse earthly bodies.

[**Musicians** *come from the house and disappear among the trees.* **Lorenzo** *calls to them*]

Come, then. Wake the goddess Diana with a hymn! With soft chords reach your mistress's ear, to call her home with music.

Jessica   I am never merry when I hear sweet music.

Lorenzo   The reason is, your spirits are attentive:
70   For do but note a wild and wanton herd,
Or race of youthful and unhandled colts,
Fetching mad bounds, bellowing and neighing loud –
Which is the hot condition of their blood;
If they but hear perchance a trumpet sound
75   Or any air of music touch their ears,
You shall perceive them make a mutual stand,
Their savage eyes turned to a modest gaze
By the sweet power of music: therefore, the poet
Did feign that Orpheus drew trees, stones, and floods,
80   Since nought so stockish, hard, and full of rage,
But music for the time doth change his nature.
The man that hath no music in himself,
Nor is not moved with concord of sweet sounds,
Is fit for treasons, stratagems, and spoils;
85   The motions of his spirit are dull as night,
And his affections dark as Erebus:
Let no such man be trusted. Mark the music.

[*Enter* **Portia** *and* **Nerissa**]

Portia   That light we see is burning in my hall.
How far that little candle throws his beams!
90   So shines a good deed in a naughty world.

Nerissa   When the moon shone, we did not see the candle.

Portia   So doth the greater glory dim the less –
A substitute shines brightly as a king,
Until a king be by, and then his state
95   Empties itself, as doth an inland brook
Into the main of waters. Music! hark!

Nerissa   It is your music, madam, of the house.

Jessica   I am never in high spirits when I hear sweet music.

Lorenzo   The reason is, your mind becomes preoccupied.
Observe a stampeding herd, or a group of young unbroken
colts, frisking about madly, bellowing and loudly neighing —
which is natural to their temperaments — if they happen to
hear a trumpet, or if any sound of music reaches their ears,
you'll see they'll all stand still, their savage eyes reduced to a
docile gaze by the sweet power of music. Therefore the poet
Ovid would have us believe that the music of Orpheus
affected trees, stones and floods. There's nothing too brutish
or stolid, or full of passion, that music won't temporarily
change its nature. The man who has no sympathy for music,
who isn't moved by melody, is fit only for treason, plotting and
mischief-making. Emotionally he's as dull as night. His
character's a dark mystery. Don't trust a man like that. Listen
to the music!

[**Portia** *and* **Nerissa** *arrive*]

Portia   [*looking toward the house*] That light we can see is
burning in my hall. How far the beams of a small candle can
travel! So shines a good deed in a corrupt world.

Nerissa   When the moon shone, we didn't see the candle.

Portia   That's because great powers diminish lesser ones. A
stand-in looks as regal as a king — until the real king comes by.
Then his importance diminishes: like an inland brook does
when it reaches the sea. [*She pauses to listen*] Music! Listen!

Nerissa   They are your own musicians, madam, from your
house.

Portia   Nothing is good, I see, without respect:
Methinks it sounds much sweeter than by day.

100 **Nerissa**   Silence bestows that virtue on it, madam.

Portia   The crow doth sing as sweetly as the lark
When neither is attended; and I think
The nightingale, if she should sing by day
When every goose is cackling, would be thought
105   No better a musician than the wren.
How many things by season seasoned are
To their right praise and true perfection.
Peace, ho! the moon sleeps with Endymion,
And would not be awaked.

[*Music ceases*]

Lorenzo   That is the voice,
110   Or I am much deceived, of Portia.

Portia   He knows me, as the blind man knows the cuckoo,
By the bad voice.

Lorenzo   Dear lady, welcome home.

Portia   We have been praying for our husbands' healths
Which speed we hope the better for our words.
Are they returned?

115 **Lorenzo**   Madam, they are not yet;
But there is come a messenger before,
To signify their coming.

Portia   Go in, Nerissa,
Give order to my servants that they take
No note at all of our being absent hence;
120   Nor you, Lorenzo; Jessica, nor you.

[*A tucket sounds*]

Portia How important setting is. I think it sounds much sweeter than in daylight.

Nerissa The silence gives it an advantage, madam.

Portia A crow sings as sweetly as a lark, when no one is listening. If nightingales sang by day, when every barnyard fowl is cackling, they'd be rated no better than wrens are. So many things appeal because they are in their right context. But quiet now! The moon is resting behind a cloud. [*The music stops as the light fades*]

Lorenzo [*listening in the darkness*] That is the voice – or I am much mistaken – of Portia!

Portia [*revealing herself*] He knows me just as the blind man knows the cuckoo – by the awful voice!

Lorenzo Dear lady, welcome home.

Portia We've been praying for the welfare of our husbands. Our words should speed them on their way. Have they returned?

Lorenzo Madam, not yet. But a messenger came ahead of them to announce their arrival.

Portia Go in, Nerissa. Order my servants to say absolutely nothing about our absence from here. Nor must you, Lorenzo; Jessica, nor you! [*She puts her finger to her lips to indicate a secret*]

[*A trumpet sounds* **Bassanio**'*s personal call*]

Lorenzo   Your husband is at hand, I hear his trumpet.
We are no tell-tales, madam; fear you not.

Portia   This night methinks is but the daylight sick,
It looks a little paler: 'tis a day,
125   Such as the day is when the sun is hid.

[*Enter* **Bassanio, Antonio, Gratiano,** *and their followers*]

Bassanio   We should hold day with the Antipodes,
If you would walk in absence of the sun.

Portia   Let me give light, but let me not be light,
For a light wife doth make a heavy husband,
130   And never be Bassanio so for me.
But God sort all. You are welcome home, my lord.

Bassanio   I thank you, madam. Give welcome to my friend.
This is the man, this is Antonio,
To whom I am so infinitely bound.

135 **Portia**   You should in all sense be much bound to him,
For, as I hear, he was much bound for you.

Antonio   No more than I am well acquitted of.

Portia   Sir, you are very welcome to our house:
It must appear in other ways than words,
140   Therefore I scant this breathing courtesy.

Gratiano   By yonder moon I swear you do me wrong,
In faith I gave it to the judge's clerk.
Would he were gelt that had it for my part,
Since you do take it, love, so much at heart.

145 **Portia**   A quarrel, ho, already! what's the matter?

Gratiano   About a hoop of gold, a paltry ring
That she did give to me, whose posy was

Lorenzo   Your husband is nearby. I recognize his trumpet. [*Winking*] We are not telltales, madam. Don't worry.

[*The cloud passes by. It is moonlight again*]

Portia   This night seems more like daylight when it's sick. It is only a little paler. It's like one of those days when the sun doesn't come out.

[**Bassanio, Antonio** *and* **Gratiano,** *with their followers, arrive*]

Bassanio   If you make a habit of walking about at night, we'll be having day at the same time as people in the Antipodes!

Portia   Let me spread light, but not my favors! A promiscuous wife makes a heavy-hearted husband. May Bassanio never be that for me. But God's will be done! Welcome home, my lord!

[**Gratiano** *and* **Nerissa** *talk separately*]

Bassanio   Thank you, madam. Welcome my friend, too. This is the man – this is Antonio – to whom I am so infinitely indebted.

Portia   You should be indebted to him in every respect. I hear he almost paid a debt for you.

Antonio   Not more than I was glad to pay.

Portia   Sir, you are very welcome to our house. There are better ways of showing it than mere words. I'll not waste breath on compliments.

Gratiano   [*to* **Nerissa;** *they have been arguing about the ring*] By the moon above, I swear you do me an injustice! Honestly, I gave it to the judge's clerk. May he lose his manhood for all I care, since you take it so much to heart, my love!

Portia   [*overhearing*] What, a quarrel already? What's the matter?

Gratiano   It's about a circle of gold, a paltry ring she gave me,

       For all the world like cutler's poetry
       Upon a knife, 'Love me, and leave me not.'

150 **Nerissa**   What talk you of the posy or the value?
       You swore to me when I did give it you
       That you would wear it till your hour of death,
       And that it should lie with you in your grave.
       Though not for me, yet for your vehement oaths,
155   You should have been respective and have kept it.
       Gave it to a judge's clerk! no, God's my judge,
       The clerk will ne'er wear hair on's face that had it.

160 **Gratiano**   He will, an if he live to be a man.

   Nerissa   Ay, if a woman live to be a man.

   Gratiano   Now, by this hand, I gave it to a youth,
       A kind of boy, a little scrubbed boy,
       No higher than thyself, the judge's clerk,
       A prating boy, that begged it as a fee.
       I could not for my heart deny it him.

165 **Portia**   You were to blame, I must be plain with you,
       To part so slightly with your wife's first gift,
       A thing stuck on with oaths upon your finger,
       And riveted with faith unto your flesh.
       I gave my love a ring, and made him swear
170   Never to part with it, and here he stands;
       I dare be sworn for him he would not leave it,
       Nor pluck it from his finger, for the wealth
       That the world masters. Now, in faith, Gratiano,
       You give your wife too unkind cause of grief.
175   And 'twere to me, I should be mad at it.

   Bassanio   [*aside*] Why, I were best to cut my left hand off,
       And swear I lost the ring defending it.

with an inscription on it like a cutler's verse on a knife: "Love me and don't part with me."

Nerissa   Why talk about the inscription or the value? When I gave it to you, you promised you would wear it till you died, and that you'd take it with you to your grave. If not for my sake, if only because of your passionate vows, you should have been more careful with it and kept it. Gave it to a judge's clerk! No, as God's my judge! – the clerk that had that ring won't ever need to shave!

Gratiano   He will, if he lives to be a man.

Nerissa   Oh, yes – if a woman lives to be a man!

Gratiano   Now on my honor! I gave it to a youth. A sort of boy. A little, well-scrubbed boy. The same height as yourself. A chatterbox of a boy, who begged it as a fee. I could not deny it to him, for all my heart.

Portia   You were to blame – I must be frank with you – in parting so lightly with your wife's first gift. It was put on your finger with vows, and riveted to your flesh with trust. I gave my love a ring, and made him swear never to part with it. Here he stands. I'll vouch he wouldn't leave it, or pull it from his finger, for all the money in the world. Now truly, Gratiano, you've given your wife an unkind cause for grief. If it were I, I'd be furious.

Bassanio   [*aside*] Why, I'd better cut my left hand off, and swear I lost the ring defending it.

Gratiano   My Lord Bassanio gave his ring away
Unto the judge that begged it, and indeed
180   Deserved it too; and then the boy, his clerk,
That took some pains in writing, he begged mine:
And neither man nor master would take aught
But the two rings.

Portia   What ring gave you, my lord?
Not that, I hope, which you received of me.

185 **Bassanio**   If I could add a lie unto a fault,
I would deny it; but you see my finger
Hath not the ring upon it, it is gone.

Portia   Even so void is your false heart of truth!
By heaven, I will ne'er come in your bed
Until I see the ring.

190 **Nerissa**   Nor I in yours.
Till I again see mine.

Bassanio   Sweet Portia,
If you did know to whom I gave the ring,
If you did know for whom I gave the ring,
And would conceive for what I gave the ring,
195   And how unwillingly I left the ring,
When naught would be accepted but the ring,
You would abate the strength of your displeasure.

Portia   If you had known the virtue of the ring,
Or half her worthiness that gave the ring,
200   Or your own honour to contain the ring,
You would not then have parted with the ring.
What man is there so much unreasonable,
If you had pleased to have defended it
With any terms of zeal, wanted the modesty
205   To urge the thing held as a ceremony?
Nerissa teaches me what to believe:
I'll die for't but some woman had the ring.

Gratiano   Lord Bassanio gave his ring away, to the judge who begged it from him, and deserved it too. And then the boy, his clerk, who took so much trouble with the documents, he begged mine. Neither the assistant nor the master would take anything but the two rings.

Portia   [*turning to* **Bassanio**] What ring did you give, my lord? Not, I hope, the one I gave to you?

Bassanio   If I could add a lie to a fault, I'd deny it. But you can see my finger is without your ring. It has gone.

Portia   [*turning away*] And your false heart is without faithfulness. By heaven, I'll not sleep with you until I see that ring!

Nerissa   [*to* **Gratiano**] Nor will I sleep with you till I see mine again.

Bassanio   Sweet Portia! If you knew to whom I gave the ring, if you knew *for* whom I gave the ring and could understand the reason *why* I gave the ring – and knew how unwillingly I parted with the ring when nothing was acceptable besides the ring – you wouldn't be so angry!

Portia   If you had known the significance of the ring, or half the worthiness of she who gave the ring, or your own obligation to retain the ring – you would not then have parted with the ring! No man would be so unreasonable, so lacking in sensitivity, as to insist on something of sentimental value, if you had been bothered to defend it with enthusiasm. Nerissa has got it right – upon my life, some woman has that ring.

Bassanio   No, by my honour, madam, by my soul,
No woman had it, but a civil doctor,
210 Which did refuse three thousand ducats of me,
And begged the ring, the which I did deny him,
And suffered him to go displeased away;
Even he that had held up the very life
Of my dear friend. What should I say, sweet lady?
215 I was enforced to send it after him,
I was beset with shame and courtesy,
My honour would not let ingratitude
So much besmear it. Pardon me, good lady,
For by these blessed candles of the night,
220 Had you been there, I think you would have begged
The ring of me to give the worthy doctor.

Portia   Let not that doctor e'er come near my house.
Since he hath got the jewel that I loved,
And that which you did swear to keep for me,
225 I will become as liberal as you;
I'll not deny him any thing I have,
No, not my body, nor my husband's bed:
Know him I shall, I am well sure of it.
Lie not a night from home. Watch me, like Argus.
230 If you do not, if I be left alone,
Now, by mine honour, which is yet mine own,
I'll have that doctor for my bedfellow.

Nerissa   And I his clerk; therefore be well advised
How you do leave me to mine own protection.

235 **Gratiano**   Well, do you so: let not me take him then,
For if I do, I'll mar the young clerk's pen.

Antonio   I am th'unhappy subject of these quarrels.

Portia   Sir, grieve not you – you are welcome
notwithstanding.

Bassanio   On my honor, no, madam! On my soul, no woman
had it! I gave it to a doctor of law. He turned down my three
thousand ducats and begged for the ring. I said no and let
him leave displeased, though he was the very man who had
saved the life of my dear friend. What can I say, sweet lady? I
was forced to send it on to him. I was filled with shame, owing
him a courtesy. My honor could not be tainted with such
gross ingratitude. With respect, dear lady, by the stars above,
had you been there I think you would have begged the ring
from me, to give it to the worthy doctor.

Portia   That doctor had better not come near my house! But
since he has the jewel I loved, and which you swore to keep for
me, I'll be as generous as you. I won't deny him anything I
have. Neither my body, nor my husband's bed. I'll get to know
him intimately! Watch me as Argus-with-the-hundred-eyes
watched Ion! If you don't, if I'm left alone, by my honor
(which is mine to give) I'll have that doctor for a bedfellow!

Nerissa   And I'll have his clerk! Therefore take care you don't
leave me to my own devices!

Gratiano   Well, go on then! But don't let me catch him, for if I
do, I'll ruin the young clerk's pen!

Antonio   I am the unhappy subject of these quarrels . . .

Portia   Sir, don't you worry. You are welcome, nevertheless.

Bassanio   Portia, forgive me this enforced wrong,
240   And in the hearing of these many friends
I swear to thee, even by thine own fair eyes
Wherein I see myself –

Portia   Mark you but that!
In both my eyes he doubly sees himself:
In each eye, one. Swear by your double self,
And there's an oath of credit.

245 **Bassanio**   Nay, but hear me.
Pardon this fault, and by my soul I swear,
I never more will break an oath with thee.

Antonio   I once did lend my body for his wealth,
Which but for him that had your husband's ring
250   Had quite miscarried. I dare be bound again,
My soul upon the forfeit, that your lord
Will never more break faith advisedly.

Portia   Then you shall be his surety. Give him this
And bid him keep it better than the other.

255 **Antonio**   Here, Lord Bassanio, swear to keep this ring.

Bassanio   By heaven, it is the same I gave the doctor!

Portia   I had it of him: pardon me, Bassanio,
For by this ring the doctor lay with me.

Nerissa   And pardon me, my gentle Gratiano,
260   For that same scrubbed boy, the doctor's clerk,
In lieu of this last night did lie with me.

Gratiano   Why, this is like the mending of highways
In summer, where the ways are fair enough.
What! are we cuckolds ere we have deserved it?

265 **Portia**   Speak not so grossly. You are all amazed:
Here is a letter, read it at your leisure;

Bassanio   Portia, forgive me this wrong, which was forced on me. With our friends as witnesses, I swear to you, by those fair eyes of yours in which I see myself reflected –

Portia   Note that! In both my eyes he sees himself duplicated! One in each eye! Swear by your two-timing self – that's a trustworthy oath!

Bassanio   [*desperate*] No, just listen to me. Pardon this fault, and I swear by my soul that I'll never again break a promise to you.

Antonio   [*coming to his aid*] I once loaned my body to obtain his happiness. But for the man who has your husband's ring, I'd have lost my life. Now I'll venture to be guarantor again, my soul this time as forfeit, that your husband will never again be persuaded to break faith.

Portia   Then you shall be his surety. [*She takes the ring from her finger*] Give this to him, and tell him to keep it better than the other.

Antonio   Here, Lord Bassanio, swear to keep this ring.

Bassanio   By heavens, it's the one I gave the doctor!

Portia   I obtained it from him. Forgive me, Bassanio. In return for this ring, the doctor slept with me.

Nerissa   [*also showing a ring*] And forgive me, gentle Gratiano. That well-scrubbed boy, the doctor's clerk, lay with me last night on payment of this ring.

Gratiano   Why, this is like repairing roads in summer, taking remedial action when it isn't necessary. What, are we to have unfaithful wives before we have deserved them?

Portia   Don't be so indelicate! [*She decides to explain*] You are all astonished. Here is a letter [*she produces one*] which you

It comes from Padua, from Bellario.
There you shall find that Portia was the doctor,
Nerissa there, her clerk. Lorenzo here
270 Shall witness I set forth as soon as you,
And even but now returned; I have not yet
Entered my house. Antonio, you are welcome,
And I have better news in store for you
Than you expect: unseal this letter soon,
275 There you shall find three of your argosies
Are richly come to harbour suddenly.
You shall not know by what strange accident
I chanced on this letter.

Antonio   I am dumb!

Bassanio   Were you the doctor, and I knew you not?

280 **Gratiano**   Were you the clerk that is to make me cuckold?

Nerissa   Ay, but the clerk that never means to do it,
Unless he live until he be a man.

Bassanio   Sweet doctor, you shall be my bedfellow:
When I am absent, then lie with my wife.

285 **Antonio**   Sweet lady, you have given me life and living;
For here I read for certain that my ships
Are safely come to road.

Portia   How now, Lorenzo?
My clerk hath some good comforts too for you.

Nerissa   Ay, and I'll give them him without a fee.
290 There do I give to you and Jessica,
From the rich Jew, a special deed of gift,
After his death, of all he dies possessed of.

Lorenzo   Fair ladies, you drop manna in the way
Of starved people.

can read at leisure. It comes from Padua, from Bellario. In it you will learn that I, Portia, was the doctor and Nerissa there was the clerk. Lorenzo here will confirm I left as soon as you did, and returned just now. I haven't yet entered my house. Antonio, you are welcome. And I have better news for you than you are expecting. [*Producing another letter*] Open this letter soon. You'll learn that three of your merchant ships reached harbor unexpectedly, richly laden. How I stumbled on this letter is a secret.

Antonio   I'm speechless!

Bassanio   [*to* **Portia**] Were you the doctor, and I didn't recognize you?

Gratiano   [*to* **Nerissa**] Were you the clerk that fancied an affair behind my back?

Nerissa   Yes, but a clerk that never intends to do it — unless he lives long enough to be a man!

Bassanio   [*to* **Portia**] Sweet doctor, you shall sleep with me. When I'm away, then sleep with my wife!

Antonio   [*having read his letter*] Sweet lady, you have given me life and a future. I read here that my ships have safely reached port.

Portia   Well, now, Lorenzo! My clerk has good news for you, too.

Nerissa   Yes, and I'll give it to him without a fee. [*She hands over the will she has prepared*] Here I give to you and Jessica a special deed of gift from the rich Jew, leaving all his possessions to you after he dies.

Lorenzo   Fair ladies, you drop manna before starving people!

Portia   It is almost morning,
295   And yet I am sure you are not satisfied
        Of these events in full. Let us go in,
        And charge us there upon inter'gatories,
        And we will answer all things faithfully.

Gratiano   Let it be so. The first inter'gatory
300   That my Nerissa shall be sworn on is,
        Whether till the next night she had rather stay,
        Or go to bed now, being two hours to day:
        But were the day come, I should wish it dark,
        Till I were couching with the doctor's clerk.
305   Well, while I live I'll fear no other thing
        So sore as keeping safe Nerissa's ring.

[*Exeunt*]

Portia [*looking at the sky*] It's almost morning. I'm sure you haven't got the whole picture. Let's go indoors. You can cross-examine us there, and we'll tell you the honest truth.

Gratiano Let's do that. The first question my Nerissa will be sworn to answer is: whether she would rather wait until tomorrow night or go to bed now, when there are only two more hours to daylight. If it were dawn, I'd be wishing for night, so that I could take the doctor's clerk to bed. Well, for the rest of my life, nothing will worry me more than the safe keeping of Nerissa's ring!

[*They all enter the house, arm in arm*]

Activities

Characters

Search the text (either the original or the modern version) to find answers to the following questions. They will help you to form personal opinions about the major characters in the play. Record any relevant quotations in Shakespeare's own words.

Shylock

1 Shylock is a professional moneylender. What words and phrases in *Act 1 Scene 3* (when we first meet him) show that he
   a thinks carefully before he makes a decision
   b dislikes risk
   c resents competition when he thinks it is unfair?

2 What words in *Act 1 Scene 3* express Shylock's own view of his business ethics?

3 What do we learn from the way in which Shylock handles the request for a loan about
   a his ability in negotiation
   b his social position in Venice?

4 What do we learn about Shylock as an employer (*Act 2 Scene 2*)? List some of his good and bad points.

5 What evidence have we of Shylock's qualities
   a as a husband
   b as a father?
   Do you think he deserved Jessica's behavior toward him?

6 What sort of home was Shylock's? Find evidence from the text of his life-style.

7 Identify the speeches that show Shylock to be an emotional man. Comment on them.

8 What examples can you find of Shylock's
   a sensitivity
   b pride?

9 Read *Act 1 Scene 3* and *Act 3 Scene 1*, then list at least eight reasons why Shylock hates Antonio.

10 a What examples does Shylock give of ill-treatment at the hands of Christians?
   b What other examples can you find of insulting behavior toward him?

11 What examples can you find of the importance to Shylock of his religion? Comment on his forced conversion at the end of the trial.

12 Shylock speaks of "this merry bond" (*Act 1 Scene 3 line 170*):
   a What do you think were his motives when he made it?
   b Are his reasons for wanting to exact it (i) understandable (ii) forgivable?

13 a What reasons does Shylock give for accepting Bassanio's invitation to supper (*Act 2 Scene 5*)?
   b What has he said earlier that makes this decision surprising?
   c What reasons does he give for wanting to stay at home that night?
   d What evidence is there that he might change his mind at the last minute? Do you think he did?

14 Examine carefully Shylock's discussion with Tubal in *Act 3 Scene 1*.
   a From his first speech, what seems to distress Shylock most?
   b What distresses him most about Jessica's conduct in Genoa?
   c What does this distress tell us of his character?

Activities

15 a Why does the discussion with Tubal make Antonio's position more perilous?

b What speech in *Act 1 Scene 3* could be quoted to show that Shylock's insistence on his bond stems from Antonio's own taunts?

16 a What is the religious reason for Shylock's refusal to accept money to release Antonio from his bond (*Act 4 Scene 1*)

b What other reasons motivate him?

c Do you think he genuinely thought he had right on his side?

17 In court, Shylock presents his own case before the Duke (*Act 4 Scene 1*). Examine his arguments for a ruling in his favor, and comment on the justice (or otherwise) of each.

18 During the trial scene (*Act 4 Scene 1*), Shylock is taunted, as he is elsewhere in the play. Consider each of these incidents in the light of

a their dramatic effectiveness

b their contribution to your understanding of Shylock's character.

19 Do you think the final decision of the court is fair to Shylock?

20 In Shakespeare's day, and afterward, Jews were depicted as comic and/or villainous characters. What qualities in Shylock distinguish him from the stereotype?

Antonio

1 a Several characters in *Act 1 Scene 1* offer reasons for Antonio's melancholy. List these reasons, and identify Antonio's personal explanation for his sadness.

b What do we learn from this scene of Antonio's

i standing in society?

ii generosity?

iii capacity for friendship?

2 Shylock has his own opinion of Antonio. What is it?

3 When Shylock and Antonio are together in *Act 1 Scene 3*, the latter's antisemitic behavior is described and acted out.

a Identify the relevant speeches and comment on them.

b How does this scene reveal another side of Antonio's character besides the melancholy one?

4 What do we learn from *Act 2 Scene 8* and *Act 3 Scene 2* of

a the relationship between Antonio and Bassanio?

b the loyalty of his Venetian friends?

List the references to Antonio's virtues.

5 a Compare the Antonio of *Act 3 Scene 3* with that of *Act 1 Scene 3*, and comment on the differences.

b Do you accept Antonio's own explanation for Shylock's hatred?

6 a In the trial scene (*Act 4 Scene 1*), what is the stance Antonio adopts in the face of Shylock's suit before the Duke?

b Examine his speeches before the entry of Portia, and say how his attitude relates to his former style of behavior.

7 Consider Antonio's last speech before Portia pronounces judgment.

a In what ways is it consistent with his character?

b Does it tell us any more about his qualities?

8 a How does Antonio respond to Portia's appeal for mercy toward Shylock?

b Comment on the terms of his proposed settlement.

9 In what way is the subplot of the ring dependent on the success of Shakespeare's portrayal of Antonio?

10 The play is named after Antonio, and he plays a central role in the development of the plot.

a Identify his connections with the other principal characters and the action of the play and b Collect expressions of approval and disapproval of his personal qualities.

c Assess the degree to which Shakespeare is successful in establishing him as an individual in his own right.

Portia

1 What do we learn of Portia in *Act 1 Scene 1* before we meet her for the first time in *Scene 2*?

2 The first words of Portia echo the first words of Antonio.

   a What is Portia's expressed grievance?

   b What evidence is there in her review of the suitors that her opening words are not a faithful reflection of her true character?

3 List the suitors reviewed in *Act 1 Scene 2* and from Portia's word portraits identify

   a her wit

   b her shrewd intelligence.

   What do we learn from this scene of Portia's sense of duty and honor?

4 Consider how she treats her various suitors – the Prince of Morocco (*Act 2 Scenes 1 and 7*), the Prince of Arragon (*Act 2 Scene 9*), and Bassanio (*Act 3 Scene 2*).

   a How does each impose a strain upon her, and reveal an aspect of her character?

   b Compare her manner during the casket scenes with her private behavior with Nerissa. What does this reveal of her personal qualities?

5 How does Portia treat (*a*) Nerissa, (*b*) her servant, in *Act 2 Scene 9*? Deduce some character traits from these relationships.

6 Portia's speeches at the beginning of *Act 3 Scene 2* tells us a great deal about her inner conflicts and feelings. What is so revealing about what she says?

7 a What do we learn of Portia's character from her first speech after Bassanio chooses the right casket? (*Act 3 Scene 2 lines 149–75*)

   b What do we learn from her response to the news of Antonio's dangerous predicament? (*Act 3 Scene 2 lines 242–320*)

8 Show from an examination of *Act 3 Scene 4* that Portia is
   a modest and
   b a capable organizer.

9 Portia's procedure in the trial scene (*Act 4 Scene 1*) is skillfully planned.
   a On what is her first appeal to Shylock based?
   b When this fails, what is her next approach?
   c In which speech, and at what point in the trial, does she appeal to Shylock on both grounds simultaneously?

10 Shylock says at one point in *Act 4 Scene 1*, "We trifle time."
   a What, in this interval, do we learn of Portia's sense of humor?
   b How does the lengthy pause they provide give her an advantage when she takes up the case again?
   c What lines show that she can turn Shylock's own words against herself?

11 After her skillful handling of the court case
   a How does she skillfully obtain the ring from Bassanio? (*Act 4 Scene 1 lines 421–5*)
   b What do you think were her motives?

12 The drama of the court scene had its beginnings in Shylock's "merry sport." The play ends with merry sport of a more genuine kind.
   a How does Portia show her mischievous sense of humor in handling the affair of the rings? (*Act 5 Scene 1 lines 165–278*)
   b Do you agree that she teases her husband in a way that is amusing but never unkind? Why or why not?

c Portia considerately brings the joke to an end when Antonio intervenes on Bassanio's behalf. What does this tell us of her sensitivity?

Bassanio

1 Look up the first words Bassanio utters in the play (*Act 1 Scene 1 line 66*). Then
  a assess them as indicators of one aspect of his character
  b trace further evidence of Bassanio's liking for revelry.

2 Bassanio twice comments on the character of Gratiano: in *Act 1 Scene 1 lines 114–18*, and *Act 2 Scene 2 lines 164–73*. What do we learn of Bassanio himself, by inference, from these criticisms?

3 Bassanio could be criticized for his way of life prior to his appeal to Antonio for a loan. Find the speech in *Act 1 Scene 1* where he confesses his shortcomings.

4 a Several characters – Antonio, Gratiano, Lancelot Gobbo, Nerissa, Solanio and Lorenzo – speak well of Bassanio or show him respect. Search the text for examples to show that he is a worthy husband for Portia.
  b How can we tell from Portia's own words that Bassanio has admirable qualities?

5 Antonio is senior to Bassanio, and a successful businessman.
  a What words in *Act 1 Scene 3* suggest that Bassanio might be the shrewder of the two?
  b Which speech in *Act 3 Scene 2* might confirm that Bassanio is indeed worldly-wise?

6 Why does Bassanio choose the leaden casket, and what does it tell us of his character?

7 Considering the vow Bassanio makes about the ring in *Act 3 Scene 2 lines 184–6*:
  a Was he right to part with it?

    b Why did he part with it?

    c Do you think his parting with it (*Act 4 Scene 1 lines 448–50*) reveals anything about his character?

8 a What evidence is there in *Act 3 Scene 2* to show that Bassanio's affection for Antonio is genuine?

    b Show how the trial scene (*Act 4 Scene 1*) bears this out.

9 What examples in the text can you find to suggest the view that Bassanio is always honest and frank?

10 Note what "the Christian husbands" say in *Act 4 Scene 1 lines 279–84 and 287–9*. Shylock disapproves. Do you?

Gratiano

1 In *Act 1 Scene 1* Gratiano deliberately contrasts himself with the melancholy Antonio.

    a Which speech best illustrates this?

    b How do his concluding words reveal that Gratiano knows some of his own faults?

    c Is Bassanio's comment on the speech a just one?

2 Bassanio is also critical of Gratiano in *Act 2 Scene 2 lines 164–73*:

    a What is the substance of his criticism?

    b Gratiano makes a long-term promise (*lines 174–82*). Does he keep it?

    c He makes a short-term exception. What does this tell us of his character?

3 Which of Gratiano's words in *Act 2 Scene 6* suggest there is a serious side to his outlook on life?

4 Gratiano's involvement in the trial scene (*Act 4 Scene 1*) is full of feeling.

    a Consider his behavior before Portia rescues Antonio and

    b after it.

    Has Gratiano changed since he first defined his philosophy of life at the beginning of the play?

5 In what ways is Gratiano's reaction to the matter of the ring different from Bassanio's?

6 Shylock says to Gratiano: "Repair thy wit, good youth, or it will fall / To cureless ruin." (*Act 4 Scene 1 lines 141-2*)

a Portia also rebukes him for coarseness in *Act 5 Scene 1*. Find this, and other examples of Gratiano's lack of refinement in his wit.

b What might have been Shakespeare's reason for giving him the last words in the play?

Nerissa

1 What can we deduce from *Act 1 Scene 2* of
a Nerissa's relationship with her mistress, Portia?
b her intelligence and commonsense?

2 What evidence is there of Nerissa's loyalty to Portia in the matter of her engagement to Gratiano?

3 What line in *Act 3 Scene 2* suggests that Nerissa might be a compliant wife?

4 What indications are there in *Act 5 Scene 1* that she will, in fact, stand up to her husband with some spirit?

5 How do we know how tall she is?

Jessica

1 From the short scene in which Jessica first appears (*Act 2 Scene 3*) find
a evidence of her generosity
b evidence of her sense of guilt
c evidence of her independence of thought
d evidence of her suppressed high spirits.

2 From her second appearance (*Act 2 Scene 6 lines 29–50*), comment on
a her modesty

b her disloyalty to her father

c Lorenzo's character study of her.

3 What evidence is there in the text of the kind of life Jessica had led prior to her love affair with Lorenzo?

4 Comment on Jessica's behavior in Genoa, as reported by Tubal in *Act 3 Scene 1*.

5 Consider Jessica's discussion with Lancelot Gobbo in *Act 3 Scene 5 lines 1–21*. Do you think she takes his words seriously, or is she amused by them?

6 What does the literary contest between Jessica and Lorenzo (*Act 5 Scene 1*) tell us about

a her wit?

b her education?

Do you think she would have won, as she claimed, but for the interruption?

7 How does music affect Jessica?

8 Jessica says that "love is blind." Does this explain behavior which the modern playgoer might deplore?

Lorenzo

1 To an Elizabethan, which speech in *Act 2 Scene 4* would excuse Lorenzo's collaboration with Jessica in her theft of Shylock's money?

2 What evidence is there of his sensitive and artistic nature, in *Act 5 Scene 1*?

3 Comment on Lorenzo's

a assessment of Jessica's virtues in *Act 2 Scene 6 lines 52–7* and

b his last words in the play.

Structure

1 There are four main stories in *The Merchant of Venice*:
a the story of Antonio, Bassanio, Shylock and the bond
b the story of Portia and the caskets
c the story of Lorenzo and Jessica
d the story of the rings
    i In what ways are *a* and *b* interlinked?
    ii What is the connection of *c* to *a* and *b*?
    iii When does story *a* begin and end?
    iv When does story *b* begin and end?
    v When does story *d* begin and end?
    vi Each of the stories *a* to *c* is introduced to the audience by means of an explanatory speech. Identify them.
    vii How is story *d* initiated? Do you think Portia planned it?

2 In addition to the four main stories, there are two simpler ones:
e the story of Lancelot Gobbo and his change of employer
f the story of Gratiano and Nerissa
    i Which of the stories *a* to *d* are linked with story *e*, and in what way?
    ii How does story *f* connect with *a* to *d*?

3 Contrast is used for dramatic effectiveness: for example, the hatred of Shylock is contrasted with the love between Bassanio and Portia.
a How many more such contrasts can you identify, and what do they add to your understanding of the play?
b *Act 5*, in contrast with the other four, has only one scene. In what ways are its mood and atmosphere different too?

Themes

1 *Love* is a theme which occurs in several of the stories. Identify which, and list those involved.

2 *Hatred* is prime motivator in the bond plot. How does it manifest itself?

3 *Friendship* is central to the play. In what respects?

4 *Money* – its uses and abuses – is a recurrent theme. Trace where it is of significance.

5 *Courtship and marriage* occupy much of the play. What view of it is portrayed?

6 *Parent/child relationships* have considerable importance. Find three, and establish their importance.

7 *Mercy* is a quality closely scrutinized. In what ways is it related to the play's moments of tension?

8 *Loyalty* binds several of the characters together. Where is it mainly manifested?

9 *Justice* is a central issue. Does Shakespeare weigh the scales evenly?

10 *Choice* is a keystone of the play. It confronts many characters. See how many instances you can find.

Setting

Venice is part of the play's title, and Shakespeare's theater had neither costumes nor scenery to help the audience to make an imaginative journey there.

1 What words in the discussion between Antonio, Salerio and Solanio which opens the play establish Venice as a rich mercantile center?

2 When Shylock explains what he means by "a good man" in *Act I Scene 3*, he describes a trading area and places Venice at a distance from England. How would this speech help an audience to feel that the action of the play is abroad?

3 In *Act 2 Scene 8*, and also in *Act 2 Scene 9*, Salerio makes geographical references which establish England as a distant place. Trace these.

4 There are at least three local details in the play which relate to Venice:
   a a business center is named in *Act 1 Scene 3*
   b a means of transport within the city is used (*Act 2 Scene 8*)
   c an intercity means of transport is mentioned in *Act 3 Scene 4*. Identify each.

5 Old Gobbo's present (*Act 2 Scene 2 line 120*) is a Venetian dish. What is it?

6 There are several references in the play to the political constitution of Venice: find the relevant passages in *Act 3 Scene 2*, *Act 3 Scene 3*, and *Act 4 Scene 1*. Why was the city so attractive to traders?

Close Reading

Read the original Shakespeare and (if necessary) the modern transcription to gain an understanding of the speeches and extracts below. Then concentrate entirely on the original in answering the questions.

1 *Let me play the fool* (*Act 1 Scene 1 line 79*)

   a This is an amusing set speech in which Gratiano makes out a case for lighthearted living rather than sober restraint. How many contrasting words and concepts can you find in the first eight lines?

   b Which of these words refer to temperature, and why?

   c Which of Gratiano's words lend themselves to being acted out rather than simply spoken? If you were directing the play, what recommendations would you make to the actor about gestures and tone of voice?

   d Which two lines (not consecutive) give the impression that Gratiano is a chatterbox who knows how to time his monologs?

   e Gratiano uses a simile in his description of those who are "reputed wise." Later, he uses an extended metaphor to clinch his point. Identify both, and show the connection between them.

2 *I will buy with you, sell with you, talk with you, walk with you, and so following: but I will not eat with you, drink with you, nor pray with you* (*Act 1 Scene 3 lines 30–33*)

   a This is a prose passage. Does it nevertheless have a rhythm, and if so, to what purpose?

   b In the first half of Shylock's declaration, there are four statements, in two pairs. Comment on what binds them together.

   c **What Shylock will not do is expressed in three parts,
each one clear and emphatic.**

     (i) Comment on the key words.

     (ii) Say why the speech would not be so effective if the
second half came first.

3 *Signior Antonio, many a time and oft (Act 1 Scene 3 line 104)*

   a Shylock's speech begins calmly and deliberately: where
would you say this introduction ends?

   b Where does a bitter note enter into his remarks? Which
words would he emphasize?

   c Which line is the turning point in the speech, leading the
way to its development and climax?

   d What is effective about the way in which Shylock uses
direct speech to make his point against Antonio? Where
in the play does he do this again?

   e Antonio is accused of three taunts and insults against
Shylock. Two of them Shylock returns to more than
once. Which are they?

   f How does Shylock introduce a mocking tone into his
speech?

4 *To bait fish withal! If it will feed nothing else, it will feed my
revenge (Act 3 Scene 1 lines 44–5)*

   a In this speech Shylock rails against Antonio on two
counts: money and religion. Where does the division
come in the speech?

   b Some critics have deplored the fact that Shylock puts
money before religion. Others have seen this as credit-
able: better that he should hate Antonio on business
grounds than because of a religious difference. Which
interpretation do you favor, and why?

   c Which verbs are emphasized in the section devoted to
money?

   d Why is Shylock's passion conveyed so effectively by
means of a series of questions? How many does he put?

e Some questions form simple sentences. Others are collected together. Discuss the effectiveness of each method of appealing to his listeners.

f Shylock uses his questions challengingly and progressively. What is gained by (i) the "tickle"/"poison" sequence and (ii) the "wrong"/"revenge" sequence?

g How does Shylock answer his own questions in a way that drives home his argument?

h Why do you suppose Shakespeare switches to the entry of a servant at the end of this speech, rather than give Salerio or Solanio a reply?

5 *The quality of mercy is not strained* (Act 4 Scene 1 line 181)

a The speech is a response to Shylock's "On what compulsion must I?" How does the simile in Portia's opening sentence effectively contrast with Shylock's harsh question?

b The quality of mercy is taken from ground level to that of the divine. (i) Show how Portia takes her argument into the realms of religious conviction. (ii) Are there identifiable echoes here and later of the Lord's Prayer?

c Extract from the speech the positive statements about mercy which define it and/or describe attributes.

6 *How sweet the moonlight sleeps upon this bank* (Act 5 Scene 1 line 53)

a This scene would have been acted out in daylight at Shakespeare's Globe Theatre. Which words in Lorenzo's first two sentences are likely to have established an atmosphere of calm tranquillity?

b What letter of the alphabet predominates, and what effect does it achieve in this context?

c "Harmony" is a key word, and relates to the music Stephano has been instructed to arrange, and also to "the music of the spheres," which was believed to emanate from the stars. (i) To what sense is Lorenzo appealing here? (ii) Which words confirm this?

d (i) Which words stress man's human limitations?

  (ii) Comment on these words in contrast with those of the passage as a whole.

7 Compare each of the passages 1–6 above with the prose translations. What extra dimensions of expression do you find in the original poetry?

8 Comment on the effectiveness of Salerio's word picture in *Act 1 Scene 1* of (i) the ocean and (ii) the dangers of ship-wreck.

9 In *Act 1 Scene 1*, Bassanio appeals to Antonio for a loan. What is the effectiveness of his schoolboy reminiscence?

10 In *Act 1 Scene 2*, Portia and Nerissa talk in prose. (i) What is the purpose of this scene and (ii) is prose best suited for it?

11 Some of Shylock's most effective speeches are also in prose. Look them up, and compare them with his major speeches in dramatic verse. Have you a preference, and if so, why?

12 Prose is the natural vehicle for characters of low birth. Comment on the scenes in which Lancelot Gobbo and his father appear, and draw some conclusions about fashions in wit and humor.

13 Some critics have noted a difference in the Lancelot Gobbo who served Shylock and the Lancelot Gobbo who serves Bassanio later in the play. Read the scenes in which he appears and say whether you agree, or disagree, with Lorenzo's speech about his skills in *Act 3 Scene 5*.

14 Take the speeches of Morocco, Arragon and Bassanio one by one, and summarize the arguments that lead them to their choices.

15 Identify the scenes in the play in which music is either present or referred to. How does music relate to the overall purposes of the play?

Examination questions

1 How effectively does Shakespeare use (*a*) Lorenzo and Jessica and (*b*) the story of the rings to establish a mood of happiness after the tensions of the trial scene?

2 *The Merchant of Venice* has been described as a play of contrasts. Which three have you found to be most important and interesting?

3 To what extent should an audience feel sorry for Shylock?

4 What aspect of Portia's character (as you understand it from the evidence in the play) accounts for her decision to assume responsibility for defending Antonio?

5 What is the dramatic importance of the two casket scenes involving the Prince of Morocco and the Prince of Arragon?

6 By detailed reference to three scenes (or parts of scenes) show how Shakespeare presents Shylock as a figure of fun, a villain and a persecuted human being.

7 "They both have good and bad in them." By careful reference to the text, say to what extent you agree with this statement about Antonio and Shylock.

8 One theme of the play is that things are not always what they seem. Examine the first casket scene with this in mind, and say what other examples you have found elsewhere of appearances being deceptive.

9 To what extent is Shylock's character revealed by his dealings with (*a*) Lancelot Gobbo and (*b*) his daughter Jessica?

10 Compare and contrast life as we know of it in Belmont, with life in Venice.

Activities

11 Pretend you are Shylock describing the trial to your friend Tubal. What would you say?

12 Critics have praised the trial scene for its dramatic effectiveness but questioned whether it has a proper place in a comedy. By specific reference to the text, find evidence for both attitudes.

13 Give a detailed account of Lancelot's deception of his father and their joint appeal to Bassanio for a new job.

14 How do Portia and Nerissa relate to each other, and how do they jointly contribute to the interest of the play?

15 Though the casket story and the story of the bond appear to be quite separate, they are in fact linked in many ways. Show the connections.

16 What can be said for and against Shylock's attitude toward Antonio?

17 Money and its importance is a recurrent theme in *The Merchant of Venice*. Illustrate how it affects any two or three characters of your choice.

18 "There are good reasons for disliking Bassanio, but the best of him comes out in a crisis." How far do you agree?

19 Is the Shylock who initially lends the 3000 ducats the same man after (*a*) the elopement of Jessica and (*b*) the verdict of the court?

20 "Antonio should never have risked his life for a mere fortune-hunter." Discuss.

21 Is Act 5, with its story of the rings, an integral part of *The Merchant of Venice*, or is it a lightweight and superfluous addition to a serious play?

22 What do we learn of Portia's character from her summary of the contestants at the beginning of the play? Compare this with her words and actions after Antonio is arrested.

23 Give an account of the trial scene from Shylock's entrance to his exit so as to bring out the qualities which would be most effective in a theatrical performance.

24 It has been said that Portia is really arguing that "the law is an ass" when it is applied without discretion. Trace her conduct of the case from her arrival to Shylock's exit.

25 How does Gratiano enliven the play and make a contribution to its dramatic appeal?

26 "The three men who choose the trial by casket also choose to reveal their characters." Do you agree?

27 "*The Merchant of Venice* is several plays skillfully dovetailed into one." Show how Shakespeare's mastery of plot is in evidence in the play.

28 Is there any dramatic justification for the Gobbo scenes? What would be lost if they were omitted?

29 What adjustments must a modern audience make in order to enjoy a performance of the Elizabethan *Merchant of Venice*?

30 Could *The Merchant of Venice* be performed successfully as a four-act play? What would be lost or gained by omitting Act 5?

One-word-answer quiz

1 Which casket contained a skull, through the eye socket of which there was a scroll?

2 Who was to be Lorenzo's torchbearer at the masque?

3 What is the name of Shylock's wealthy friend?

4 For how many months did Bassanio borrow the 3000 ducats?

5 Who drew up Shylock's deed of gift?

6 What name does Portia assume to conduct Antonio's case?

7 According to Shylock, which Old Testament character did "the wise young judge" resemble?

8 Who was described as "a little scrubbed boy"?

9 What was the name of the business center in Venice?

10 In which town did Jessica spend 80 ducats?

11 Whose ring was inscribed "Love me, and leave me not"?

12 Whose "little body" was "aweary of this great world"?

13 Who chose the casket labeled "Who chooseth me shall get as much as he deserves"?

14 How many merchants pleaded with Shylock to release Antonio from his bond?

15 What was the name of the learned doctor of Padua who assisted Portia with clothes and advice?

16 What is the name of the messenger who announces the return of Portia and Nerissa?

17 What name does Gratiano give to the sort of men "whose visages do cream and mantle like a standing pond"?

18 Apart from a ring, what present did Portia accept from Bassanio at the end of the trial?

19 How many sealed bags of ducats did Jessica steal?

20 Which of Portia's suitors "did nothing but frown"?

21 Which of Portia's suitors spoke only English?

22 Who says he would like to "play the fool"?

23 Who "stood with a willow in her hand," according to Lorenzo?

24 What fraction of Shylock's goods was Antonio entitled to after the trial?

25 On which sandbank near England was one of Antonio's ships supposed to have foundered?

26 When Portia leaves for Venice, whom does she leave in charge of her home?

27 On what does Shylock whet his knife during the trial scene?

28 As Portia returns home after the trial, what does she first see at a distance?

29 What is it that Shylock says is the reason he prefers "carrion flesh" to 3000 ducats?

30 How many of Antonio's argosies came safely home to port?

31 What was the name of Shylock's deceased wife?

32 Whose "sunny locks hang on her temples like a golden fleece"?

33 Who is said to be "too wild, too rude, and bold of voice"?

34 How many rich jewels did Jessica steal from Shylock?

35 What did Jessica receive in exchange for one of the jewels?

36 Where was Portia's home situated?

37 What kind of dish did Old Gobbo bring for his son's master?

38 What was the name of Old Gobbo's horse?

39 What were Bassanio, Gratiano and Lorenzo planning on the night the wind turned?

40 According to Portia, how many times is mercy blessed?

41 What was the name of Lancelot Gobbo's mother?

42 From which city did the suitor come who bored Portia with his talk of horses?

43 Who "grazed his uncle Laban's sheep"?

44 Where does Portia pretend she is going when she leaves home to save Antonio?

45 What was the name of the imaginary ship that worried Salerio whenever he saw an hourglass?

46 Which of Portia's suitors was dark of hue?

47 *Act 5 Scene 1* takes place in what kind of light?

48 Which casket bore the legend "Who chooseth me shall gain what many men desire"?

49 What did the fiend advise Lancelot to do?

What's missing?

Complete the following quotations:

1 All that glisters is not gold . . .
2 'I am Sir Oracle . . .'
3 Till thou canst rail the seal from off my bond . . .
4 I am glad 'tis night, you do not look on me, / For . . .
5 The fiend is at mine elbow, and tempts me, saying to me . . .
6 If I can catch him once upon the hip . . .
7 If to do were as easy as to know what were good to do . . .
8 I should not see the sandy hour-glass run . . .
9 Let music sound while he doth make his choice; / Then . . .
10 I never knew so young a body with . . .
11 I hold the world but as the world, Gratiano . . .
12 You call me misbeliever, cut-throat dog . . .
13 He doth nothing but frown, as who should say '. . .'
14 Not on thy sole, but on thy soul, harsh Jew . . .
15 Alack, what heinous sin it is in me / To be . . .
16 It is twice blest: . . .
17 I am sorry for thee, thou art come to answer . . .
18 There I have another bad match . . .
19 Why, all the boys in Venice follow him, / Crying . . .
20 But when this ring / Parts from this finger, then . . .
21 The patch is kind enough, but a huge feeder . . .
22 My meaning in saying he is a good man is . . .
23 His reasons are two grains of wheat hid in two bushels of chaff . . .

24 A diamond gone, cost me . . .

25 Mark you this, Bassanio; / The devil can . . .

26 In sooth, I know not why I am so sad . . .

27 Your wife would give you little thanks for that . . .

28 My wind, cooling my broth, / Would blow me to an ague when . . .

29 There are a sort of men whose visages . . .

30 He is well paid that . . .

31 I will buy with you, sell with you, talk with you . . .

32 The man that hath no music in himself . . .

33 What should I say to you? Should I not say . . .?

34 I know the hand; in faith, 'tis a fair hand . . .

35 In my schooldays, when I had lost one shaft . . .

36 I will not choose what many men desire, / Because . .

37 All things that are, / Are with more spirit chased . . .

38 In such a night as this . . .

39 Let me play the fool . . .

40 Mislike me not for my complexion . . .

41 In the cutting of it, if thou dost shed . . .

42 Now, by this hand, I gave it to a youth, / A kind of boy, . . .

43 You saw the mistress, I . . .

44 How many things by season season'd are . . .

45 You that choose not by the view . . .

46 You take my house when . . .

47 You taught me first to beg, and now, methinks . . .

48 How sweet the moonlight . . .

49 If every ducat in six thousand ducats / Were in six parts . . .

50 So may the outward shows be least themselves . . .

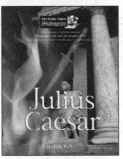

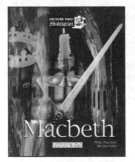

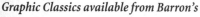